*Wishbone*

Julie Marie Wade

# Wishbone

a memoir in fractures

*Colgate University Press*
*Hamilton, New York*

First Edition 2010
10  11  12  13  14  15    6  5  4  3  2  1

The paper used in this publication meets the minimum requirements of
American National Standard for Information Sciences—Permanence of
Paper for Printed Library  Materials, ANSI Z39.48-1992.∞™

ISBN-13: 978-0-912568-21-8

**Library of Congress Cataloging-in-Publication Data**
Wade, Julie Marie.
   Wishbone : a memoir in fractures / Julie Marie Wade. — 1st ed.
      p. cm.
   Includes bibliographical references.
   ISBN 978-0-912568-21-8 (alk. paper)
   I.  Title.

   PS3623.A345W57 2010
   811'.6—dc22

                                        2010008565

Cover image by Sara J. Northerner. Used with permission.
Text and cover design by Mary Peterson Moore


*Manufactured in the United States of America*

*For my parents, without whom the Past was not possible*

   *For Angie, without whom the Present is nothing to write home about*

We don't see things as they are; we see them as we are.

≈   Anaïs Nin

# Contents

I

# Wishbone

Welcome to the floor show of the future, the life in potential. Three-ring circus: this, that, and the other. A lion tamer cracks his whip; a woman painted like a peacock descends from her trapeze. This is it. You have arrived. Welcome to the bright, shining abacus of If.

> *Moons and Junes and Ferris wheels*
> *The dizzy dancing way that you feel*
> *As every fairy tale comes real*
> *I've looked at love that way*

Once upon a time, in an orchard, on an eighteenth of June, in the presence of God and a priest and a man who must be (*must remain*) my first lover—in a sense then, also, my first love—I did not arrive. I was expected, perhaps even pined for, and I hid myself away like stolen treasure. *If love, then* . . . I had written vows; some were tender and sincere; all were tentative. *If marriage, then* . . . I know now that absence is not the answer, or even the first curled frond of the explanation. Absence is a failure of the will. *If promises, then* . . . Mine a determined disappearance, a voluntary vanishing.

Fall the first bead. Slide it over. We are counting now. The rehearsal has ended.

When I fell, twice in one year, they were concerned about the "soft spot," the fontanelle. I was four, so the most vulnerable place in my skull had long since sealed and toughened, yet my mother feared it would open again. (A worry not without warrant, it appears.) Years in the future, confessing my love for a girl, she murmured, "You've gone soft in the head again." Her fear palpable, the nuggets of her knuckles chattered.

*If only we hadn't eaten so much fish . . . The mercury you know, the madness.*
*If only we hadn't sent you to Catholic school . . . Too much time unsupervised*
     *with the Sisters.*
*If only . . . If only . . .*

I fell first from a swing, dizzy from my father's underdog. He was tall like a mountain, and I cried "Higher! Higher!," yearning to see the world from such a vantage. As he pushed harder, I pumped my legs, leaning back and stretching my toes till they tangled with the branches of the lowest trees. Then, my neck loose on my shoulders, my hair unraveling string, I looked back—all the cool sand smoothed over concrete, the broken shells. *I let go.* Not a sound escaped my lips, just the heat of a fresh flush and then the silence. A crowd gathering on the quiet promenade of Lincoln Park. My parents' frantic faces peering down. "Are you hurt? Is anything broken?" But the stunned body, the purloined speech. Pain vanishes. Did you know? I watched it recede like a wave from the shore. Over my left eye, a clot of blood, and the seagulls—so many—soaring overhead.

Then the circus: first time under the big tent: all flustered gaze and fire-eating spectacle. And the elephants, white-painted toes and glittering crowns, paraded around with their howdahs full of children. I climbed the ladder, last rider squeezed in under the silver bar. My father waving, my mother's voice above the din of strangers: "Hold on tight!" But how? But where? Nothing to cling to, and the elephant's ears flapping thick stale air, and my body coming free from its sash. I slid down the side of him, flat as a penny against his wrinkled skin, rattling the bones of my ribs. "We could sue you for this!" my mother sobbed. My father, slinging me over his back like a knapsack, my wild assemblage of limbs. I am beside myself, and then beyond: disembodied, surveying. None of the pain seeps in. No harm done. Will death be as easy? Will love?

Anger, the second bead, which is sorrow also. Anger, which is sorrow's kiln.

Before my mother began to scream, she would walk through the house shutting every window, drawing every shade. Neighbors—in her philosophy— were most tolerable when kept at a distance, in a state of amiable oblivion. Summer came, and her rage boiled like water on the stove. When the last window had been closed, she overflowed. Winter, which lacked the intermittent silence, the bracing of hands and the bowing of heads, lingered like a hair on her trigger. At any moment, the roof could cave in, the ceiling shatter. And I, so gangly and white: I quivered like a wick, ever an inch from that flame.

We had friends then, and the friends always had children. Once, I remember, we shared a cabin with the Johnsons at Ocean Shores. In the shallow glow of morning, I stumbled out of bed. Mr. Johnson was sitting on the toilet, a silhouette in blue, his pajamas down around his ankles and a comic book (those slender, raspy pages) in his hands. I stood a long time before he saw me, not embarrassed then to be staring. When his dark eyes met mine in the dim light, I said only, "Why don't you stand up like my daddy does?" and staggered back toward my borrowed room.

The next day we ate Dungeness fresh from the surf and never talked about it. A story, like the rest of my life, foreshadowed. But in the future, I would not witness so shamelessly. I would find virtue in averting my eyes.

At Seaside, another vacation, pretending to be asleep: "Please, Linda," my father whimpered. It wasn't the voice of lust speaking (a voice I would learn), but the voice of loneliness (a language already so familiar . . . ). *Please*. She wouldn't have him, and his words turned softer, more insistent. Under the blankets, I was trembling. *Never*, I thought, *will I withhold from my husband that way*.

After a while, we didn't see the Johnsons anymore. Eric, their son, jealous of his newborn sister, carried a pillow into her room while my mother and Mrs. Johnson were sipping tea, flipping through the pages of a JCPenney catalogue. I watched him slink by, one finger raised to his lips and a threat in his eyes: *Don't tell anyone, don't you dare*. His mother, sudden as instinct, jumped to her feet, scurrying away to "check on Anna." I followed. And what she found—what I saw through the triangle of light between her thighs—was Eric leaning over the crib, sobbing and smothering the baby at the same time.

There is something about being a child, about the smallness—so far below see level—that makes me shiver, even now, safe in my grown-up skin. The persistent awareness of someone looming: larger than you and with a power you wish you had. How they always noticed me when I didn't want them to—small falters, sly smiles; how they were never watching with the right eyes.

Add hunger. Add thirst.

Chelsea Brothers is beautiful. An implicit knowledge. Slip knots are difficult and roller skates are dangerous, and Chelsea, with her curly red hair and pink glasses and a trail of freckles blazing her arms, makes me hungry for cupcakes dolloped with strawberry frosting. I am in the first grade, and she is in the sixth. I won't see her again, after this year, which troubles me beyond expression. Time, really, is what poses this problem, for my sense of myself as so much older than everyone else while confined almost exclusively to same-aged companions. Even recess is segregated: fourth- through sixth-graders playing together, then afterward, first through third. And through the rain-streaked windows of Miss Campbell's class, I contemplate a future without Chelsea. Who will I study on the playground now? Who will hold my interest once she's gone?

*If only . . . If only . . .*

Mrs. Cooper is our music teacher. She wears a black lace bra under red and white silk blouses. It always shows through, especially when she stands up in front of the full auditorium to conduct our choir recitals. Her perspiration stains are also visible, but I like them because they mean she's a real person and not a robot like most adults I know. Mrs. Cooper—whose adult name is Elaine, which makes me think of lemonade on a sultry day—has glasses that leave skid marks on both sides of her nose and stringy blond hair my mother insists should be "cut and permed." And there's some kind of scandal because Mrs. Cooper has a dark-skinned son named Isaac and a husband nobody ever sees, and I understand intuitively that he is hiding . . . present but absent, just like me.

*This is your new thing now*
*Naked as a rose, everything exposed*
*But not quite*

Then the day came: I was chosen over Jason Frye to play Psalty in the end-of-school musical. The character, a life-sized blue book with felt cover, cardboard spine, and crackly accordion pages, regaled the assembled families with Bible verses and syrupy lozenges of common sense set to song.

Backstage, Mrs. Cooper prepared my transformation. Lowering the massive structure over my head, she crouched inside, fastening the harness that centered the costume square on my shoulders, drawing my arms through the narrow sleeves. "Pardon me for being so personal," she always said as she cinched the belt tighter around my beanstalk body and bent lower to lace up my shoes.

"Are you nervous?"

"Not really." But my heart was thumping like a boxer's fist inside a glove.

"I know you'll do a terrific job tonight. Just remember not to hold the microphone too close to your mouth."

But what she never knew—what I never could have told her—was how those sharp adrenaline swells had nothing to do with the performance at hand but with Mrs. Cooper's gentle and precise adjustments, the warm satisfied feeling of being touched by a woman who was not my mother or even my friend. The scent of her maple-sweet skin. Her nimble fingers with a thin gold band. Cloaked in those pages, I felt the freedom to inhabit my body differently, to move across the stage with uncustomary confidence. And afterward, when the cameras had stopped flashing and the crowd dispersed, I slid in my arms, sealed my eyes, and waited for Mrs. Cooper to release me—cramped and exhilarated—from my snug cocoon.

Ever the loneliness. Ever and always again.

All at once I knew, and there could be no convincing me otherwise: that the world, which Columbus envisioned as radical sphere, which he sailed as though it were masterable . . . this world, lauded at once as wide and small, extensive and intimate, was also arbitrary—and as such, utterly out of control.

As in *Candide*: the first musical, the interminable classic. Theodicy a window to be wriggled through, like lazy-eye blindness and tongue-less kisses. Here at hand: the inescapable evil, the untraceable God. "Best of all possible worlds" reducible to resignation.

I learned irony from a spelling bee, when the seventh-grade championship rested on "apparatus." How could it be I forgot the second "p," or that the word itself had been erased from my memory?

What would the Poet say? *The way things work is eventually something catches.*

Or its converse: *The way things work is eventually something*—someone—*is caught.*

But language is not our first language. Innuendo, insinuation, intuition. The *I*s have it—for lack of a better idiom. Betrayed by speech, misunderstandings of the medium. As in "belonging," which stands semantically for socialized acceptance. Gary Blendheim at my parents' church, tapping his cane to my pew. "When are you going to start acting out like the other kids do?"

My mouth is dry from communion wine, stumbling over the answer: "I'm always acting, Mr. Blendheim; don't you worry."

*Belonging*, with its suggestion of approval, its connotation of "blending in." Look how the syllables tell another story: *be-longing*. I can hear a hyphen in it. To be always yearning, in perpetual lack. To want what we cannot have.

And the casualties, love and war. Tell me where the casual is in those.

And God, who calls us to attention with the Nicene Creed, whose existence we accept as if a theorem. "You don't prove a theorem," my math teacher says. "You use theorems to prove Other Things."

But when the congregation stands, and my father's hands are laced behind my shoulders, our voices seem to say: *hollow would be Thy name.* "Not hollow, *hallowed*," he tries to explain, "meaning something holy, raised on high." Yet week after week, the vacuous prayer: boomerang belief, its echo.

It may be that Neil Simon ruined me with *Barefoot in the Park*, its promises of struggles that are worth it: where is the ruler for suffering, let alone its alchemy? How I thought then, *I will never marry*, and how I was right—though not for the reasons I imagined.

Or maybe it was Frank Sinatra: his falsifying blue eyes, his swindler's story.

> *The world still is the same*
> *You'll never change it*
> *As sure as the stars shine above*
> *You're nobody till somebody loves you*
> *So find yourself somebody to love*

Once upon a time, there were two sisters, Amy and Brenda. They were daughters of my mother's friend. Amy was the older one, and she lived at the back of the house in a dark room with the shades always drawn. Brenda, the younger one, kept a room above the kitchen that was flooded with light and warmed by the heat of baking. I had passed Brenda's room dozens of times, always on my way to the bathroom. It was a pleasant room with a sleigh bed made of blond wood and ceramic horses galloping across the windowsill. The soft colors, the sugary light. It was a room a child could feel safe in. But at the end of the hall and around the corner beckoned Amy's room, the door she always left a bit ajar. And I would stop and stare and wonder about the mammoth comforter slipping down to the floor and the canopy bed draped in curtains. *What must be hiding there?*

So the day came when Mrs. Edwards and my mother were busy stuffing envelopes and licking postage stamps. We would not make it home in time for my nap. Mrs. Edwards said, "Choose the bedroom upstairs you would like to sleep in. The girls are away today. They won't mind." But I was still standing beside the kitchen table. *Choose*, she had said. My fingers fidgeting, my breath in tiny gasps. *Choose.*

What I wanted, I can tell you now, was to cross the dangerous threshold into Amy's room, delve beneath those hallowed blankets. Some magic must have been lurking there—spilling from the unkempt drawers, weighty and wild behind the louvered concealment of the closet. But as I climbed the stairs, it was

Brenda's room, tidy and bright, plain as a pile of sand, which opened to me, extended itself like the pinkening palm of a hand. I chose the familiar one, timid at first in the face of those rooms, then lying awake to regret. Narnia only a doorway away, and I afraid to cross over.

Add algebra. Add geometry. The long words now, the leaner.

Figures and shapes. Calculations. Concerns about the math of the body. (Proportions.) (Ledgers of probability.) (Risk.)

And my favorite word in this whole looming language, this project of artifice: *prospect*, as in wheat that has yet to be gleaned.

A world of two dimensions morphs into three. Paper moon eclipsed, constellation of contradictions in orbit. All the origami swans and Jenga puzzles. Lines become planes with axes: X is for girls, and Y is for boys. No longer pink and blue, but something visceral, essential. Here and now, like houses that cannot stand—or built on sand—we are divided.

At the all-girls school, Xs in overload. I cannot escape the reflexive property and move on to the transitive. X = X. Does it work with other letters? I = I. But am I myself, equal to or greater than, surpassing? And the fear: I < X: Athena, the woman in me, set to rising.

> *I won't forget when Peter Pan*
> *Came to my house, took my hand,*
> *I said I was a boy, I'm glad he didn't check.*
> *I learned to fly, I learned to fight,*
> *I lived a whole life in one night*
> *We saved each other's lives out on the pirate deck.*

April, who was my friend then, in that incessant springtime, whom I loved like a sister and fellow hothouse flower, withdrew from space, her long golden tracks erasing. Soon, I could not even plot her at coordinate points. I could not pin her to any precise location. We were going to live in the city when we grew up, like Mary Richards and Rhoda Morgenstern. It was the Emerald City, and we were green—poppies more potent than we imagined. "I just want to sleep," she whispered. "Everyone keeps asking so much of me. Is it wrong to just want to be rescued?"

*Maiden.* As in *name.* As in *voyage.*

There were so many women who refused to age, sheltered there inside their parents' homes. Virgins by virtue and trade. Janet Laudan never met a man to love, despite thirty years of teaching fourth grade and faithful attendance at church. For my Aunt Linda, it was also the same. And this burden: the prospect and the honor unclaimed, the shrinking cellophane of the ever-camouflaged body.

My mother said, "maidenhead," but I heard pain. And we were supposed to be guarding it, with our tridents and our pitchforks raised.

I wished then for the missing Y, for the question that would carry its own answer. Two-pronged seemed the masculine way: physical strength plus transparency. In poems, I was always George Bailey. I could dance the jitterbug and lasso the moon. I made girls like Mary Hatch and Violet Bick swoon. Even George Bailey said: "I don't want to get married, ever, to anyone, do you understand? I want to do what *I* want to do." But in time, I = Y and Y = U, so I = U. The *I*s have it—and the *U*s too.

*Com.* As in *-promise.* As in *-passion.*

When I sold shoes, it was always "on commission." Not a team sport, a triathlon: this, that, and the other. Never sure till the end of the day if you had made the cut, risen up from minimum wage. (Rent—and Other Things—riding.) We did prospect research, calling the customers up on the phone, mailing out compliments attached to coupons. One day a face through a stack of boxes, the sliding ladders of circumstance. An X again, for him: pleated skirts and perfect manners. Culling forth *supposed to* from *supposition.*

X marks the spot on the treasure map. Expletives deleted from a transcript. Women like Watergate, destination unnamed but claimed by the reaching. (Documented.) (Contained.) A flag planted in sand to the rhythm of a marching band. My island-self turned peninsular. *And hollow would be my name.*

There was this comfort: living by the sea. I retreated again to the ocean, my nubile heart a net of fishes: what to hold on to, what to toss back. We had intended to honeymoon there, my husband and I, but I heard the word differently

under that sky. *Husband*, derivative of *husbandry*: careful management or con-
servation of resources. As if I were to be tended. As if to be kept like a tab.

But I wanted it too: that safety: love like a Brenda's room. Soft colors
and sugary light. Since the first baptism had been a flop, I piqued at this possibility of redemption. A fresh benediction and a new name. Rhetorical impera-
tives: *till death do us part* and *happily ever after*. Desire to belong and still be
longing.

> *Isn't it rich?*
> *Aren't we a pair?*
> *Me here at last on the ground,*
> *You in mid-air.*
> *Send in the clowns.*

Each Thanksgiving at my grandmother's house, we took turns handling the
slingshot. Brittle Y-bone with both arms raised, forked out from the hot grease
of the basted bird. That year I pulled harder than usual. Tendons snapped, a
wish intact: the long end of the stick was mine.

I thought of you then, my friend, the woman I walked with and drank with
and sometimes dreamed of when doused with a bottle of wine. Can wish =
question? Can dream = prospect? I was afraid to imagine us, louvered and lovely, uncertain as Amy's room.

*If I kiss you now, will the moat overflow? Will the castle be cut off from land?*
*If I admit I am not everything I was intended to be, will every cigarette I've ever*
  *smoked come back to burn me?*

You do the math. The string of Xs like chicken scratch, a row of stitches
sealing up the past. They won't forgive me for "breaking with tradition." My
mother, old for twenty-two, had married a shoe salesman. He worked his way
up. One day he was king of his castle. (A cuckold to criticism, curfews.) As the
saying goes, "If a man's house is his castle, let him clean it," while my mother
tends to her garden: flowers she keeps like a tab.

I thought of you then and of the great resilience of sea stars growing back arms and of ships miraculously lodged inside bottles. *How do we get where we are?* "Within" groups and also "between" them. In the interstice, the caesura, the space derived between the fabled rock and its proverbial hard place, I leaned back and inhaled the laughing gas: whole world reduced to guffaw. "You have heart-shaped bicuspids," the dentist observed, which he assured me meant nothing good or bad but just unusual.

I wondered then whether we could hover under an umbrella like that: let the rain run down, sprinkling our shoes. Descriptive, for once, not evaluative. We wouldn't need their blessings, and we wouldn't change our names—content in the end to answer to "unusual" . . .

Hope a blue bead. Blue as the sea or the sky.

I did not arrive and, in the days that followed, marveled at the course a failure takes. First, a blue bruise: grief-stricken. What of compromise now, what of compassion? When I let go, I saw the earth spinning below me, knowing there was no soft way to land. Some great illusions would have to be shattered. Some essential heart, split like a sand dollar, in two.

Then, the bruise is green and a little golden, and I remember what the Poet said: *Nature's first green is gold.* A lullaby in this language: something to console. Your bed so small we huddled all night. Incessant springtime. Trusting our best selves to bloom.

Now purple again, around the edges. When you touch it this time, a pain not possible to imagine before. Ripening like rare fruit. Not remorse exactly, but regret you don't wish otherwise; that you cannot succumb and will not be shaken. *Was it all a conspiracy? Had you taken leave of your senses?*

Every morning you wash your face and your hands. You stand a moment before the bathroom mirror, astonished. How has death been this easy? How love?

Leaving it all behind us, we cross the border into Canada. Twenty minutes north to set foot inside another country. XXOO, I mark in the sand: affection for what we have and for what we are lacking.

"It's hard to tell a story that isn't post hoc. Every outcome turns inevitable in the end."

And we portray it that way, don't we? In this best of all possible worlds, Xs and Ys might not matter so much as we suppose. And choice again—that hallowed word—deft on Mrs. Edwards's tongue. That one imperative. *Choose.*

There is a white rock at White Rock, a literal simplicity to cherish. We take a picture there for posterity, for the future we will not hand down.

A little farther up the shore, barefoot in tide pools, our shoestrings tied and slung over our shoulders, we come upon pilings latticed with a species called *Pisaster*: I recognize them from biology class: large purple and orange starfish native to the Pacific Northwest. There are dozens of them, spiny and bright, shiny as a bruise in transformation. They are hugging tight to the wood, between the barnacles and the seaweed braids.

*If only* . . . this. *If only* . . . that. I hold your hand as if there were no other.

# II

# Dreaming in Alpha

I have walked this road before, in another life, my feet less deliberate on the shiny, rain-slick streets—my eyes less certain of their destination. It is 1963, and I am not born yet. In fifteen years, someone will imagine me. In sixteen years, I will arrive in a slippery, blood-soaked dream. But for today, I am No One, non-entity in the guise of woman, wrapped up in my midwinter coat, hands stuffed deep inside my pockets to keep warm.

I am walking, and I do not know that I am dreaming, though somewhere in the deeper silence, I suspect it all along. Seattle wears a face with fewer wrinkles, a smoother stretch of cheek. Traffic flows between Seneca and James without congestion. The bright cars gleam: candy-apple, butterscotch, and tapioca. I want to call them classics, but they aren't yet: these souped-up, rag-top wonders. And see, I have wound back the clocks—or someone has—so what was once antique, today is avant-garde.

The world as I know it has changed, but I am not puzzled by the larger questions, only by a smaller one. I take out a slip of paper, crumpled in my hand, and try to remember. *Why am I here?* Always a useful question—and the memory follows. *A name.* A name sketched in purple ink and, beside it, this address. I stand still and gaze up at the building. I am a student, and I have come to visit my friend. She is a student also and lives *here*, in a sorority house on the corner of Northeast 54th Street and Pine. I have written down three Greek letters. I have no idea what they mean. I could ask my friend Kara, who studies Greek—but I haven't met her yet. I only think for a moment I have, and then I forget everything except a feeling of that former, later life. *A sidewalk-chalk impression.* I am conscious of having lived before, and in such a way that before is after, like reading the ending of a story first and then its early chapters.

I sense it, but the dream ambles forward with my feet, light and hopeful on the bony bare earth. Life as it should be . . . unexpected.

≈

A man steps out of the building as I am preparing to enter. He stands tall and looks taller because he is thin. *So thin*. Legs long as the face of a disappointed child, which he will tell me someday when we meet in my other life, but not now. His hair is black and slicked back against his head in Brylcreemed experiment. Next year it will be forcibly buzz-cut by a stocky uniformed barber, and thereafter will grow in lighter and lighter until, at the ripe age of thirty, he will turn gray—an early distinction of life that was lived, and honorable discharge, and change.

*He doesn't know this yet.*

I smile at him shyly, reflexively, the way my mother will teach me to do: politeness to conceal all fears. And I am not afraid really, but wondering about this man and what he will say and how I feel I know him already because of who he will be to me in a future neither of us can clearly perceive. He smiles back, teeth less coffee-stained than I expected: same afternoon stubble, same comforting eyes. He is not tired, not blackened around his cheekbones from the late nights calling a cat inside on the endless back porch of stagnant suburbia, from the early mornings driving to work with an uncovered cup of coffee in his hand, praying softly between breaths of a speaker on a motivational tape and the lurches of his headstrong car. He has not been burned yet. I can see in his confident, still-schoolboy steps: he has not been burned.

≈

"Don't I know you from somewhere?" the young man asks, pausing on the stair and looking back at me with a glint of recognition in his eyes: pale blue, watery, sincere.

"Me?" Surprised by the sound of my own voice . . .

"Are you in Dr. Callahan's business class?"

"I don't think so," I tell him haltingly. "*No.* I'm an English major."

"That's strange," he says, still appraising me in a friendly, curious way. "I swear I've seen you somewhere before. Do you live here?"

I look up at the house, its magnificent letters etched in stone, its tidy blue awnings draped down from second-story windows like aprons over the knees of a fair-skinned maid. "No, not here," I say. "I'm from Seattle, though—West side."

And he smiles and tells me in happy, eager tones that he is from the West side, too. He had grown up there, on 40th Avenue between Trenton and Donovan. I tell him I know it well, that I live two blocks away in a little brick house with a view of the water. 42nd Street. *Funny we've never met.* I want to tell him that in 1974 he will buy the house where I live now. He will convert the carport to a red garage and fall from the roof cleaning gutters on a summer afternoon; that he will lie on the sofa with his leg in a cast, watching ferryboats with their easy glide across the Bay, and back again, and he will envy them their freedom. And one night, years later, while his wife sits awake in the kitchen, drafting their lives on steno paper—while his daughter lies fitfully sleeping in her canopy princess bed—he will stand in the living room of that house on 42nd Street, staring through the window and realizing with a sad, disconsolate breath that the ferryboats aren't free at all. Theirs a prescribed journey, leaving and returning at designated hours, from Blake to Southworth and again to Fauntleroy, where they wait for the next cargo load, next foghorn, next departure. But I look into his clear cornflower eyes and permit him to dream a little longer of sailboats and Sunday evenings wasted on a windstorm, of a woman he could love between deep kisses and free-flowing hair. That woman is not my mother, and "Yes," I say, "West Seattle is lovely this time of year."

He nods and sticks out his hand—un-ringed, un-weathered—still large enough to clasp my fingers tight inside his cherry-young palm, and this man whom I will someday love in a later life tells me his name: "I'm Bill Wade. It's good to meet you," and I, having no name but the name he will give me, reply, "I'm Julie," and he smiles.

≈

Up the stairs inside the sorority house with the blue-apron windows my friend is waiting. She sits in the lounge with her thick black hair twisted into peace braids and patchwork pants that make me think, for a moment, of Oz. "You look different," I say to Vanessa, remembering her with a shaved head and cutoff Calvin Kleins. But she ignores my words, or else she doesn't hear. Looking up instead with brown inquiring eyes, she asks, "Who was that you were talking to outside?"

"Just a man," I reply, suddenly awkward under her dissecting stare. I walk over to the window, stand with my back to the slender girl on the sofa whom I supposed I knew, but now am not so sure.

"He's in my business class," she says, even though my body insists in the tense silence that I don't want to discuss it anymore.

Then, on a whim, I ask her: "What was he doing here?" I am still facing the window, still following the Lego links of city traffic with my eyes.

"He's dating one of my sisters," she replies, nearly whispers in my ear. Vanessa is standing beside me now. I feel crowded in the cold drawing room; my neck grows warm. "A girl named Bobbi Aspen. Do you know her?"

"No, I don't think I do." But then I recall a yearbook on a coffee table, and my mother telling my father to put it away: *no point reminiscing, you can't get it back after all.* And there was a girl, yes, with a boy's name, and a beautiful, crooked smile, cherry-red lips and dark curls that could, I imagine, flow free in the wind on a stormy day. Last name like a mountain slope.

As we speak, she steps into the room. *Bobbi.* Smiles and bends down to adjust her stockings, which are slipping below her knees. Her curls are tucked up under a blue and gray tam that she might throw up at the sky the way Mary Richards will do seven winters from now on the television screen. Vanessa moves to make an introduction, but I stop her with a shake of my head and a swollen pink hand that cannot cease trembling. I've seen enough for one day.

≈

Outside I choke on the dense white air, too thick for deep breaths or clear vision. A fog is settling, and I lament the loss of my mittens that are not in my pockets where they should be . . . always have been. I am aware now in my less-than-weightless state that I am carrying a handbag on my shoulder made of blue fabric with a zipper that sticks like clenched teeth. I struggle to pry it open and find inside a package of cigarettes—soft-pack, Basics. I frown because they are not my brand and because they are unfiltered. *Do I smoke these?* I dig deeper for change and discover a bus pass, and then I am walking again, smoking and walking, under the pale blue sky. Pale blue. Watery. Surreal.

When the bus comes, I put out my cigarette with the small precise toe of my shoe. I am wobbling a little, first from confusion and now from the nicotine surge in my blood. There is a woman, young like me, or young like I think I am, and she is sitting in the first seat behind the driver, clinging tightly to the safety of a book. Her eyes dart up, flaming blue, inspect me a moment, then quickly return to the page. I am drawn to her: the dark beauty behind the plain clothes. She is not colorful but alluring in that black-and-white, old-fashioned-photograph way. I sit down beside her on the stony chair, and she adjusts her umbrella—nervous, I think, that I am sitting so close, and wondering why I have chosen to sit *here of all places*, and it is strange because I am wondering the very same thing.

≈

"Good book?" I inquire, but she can't seem to decide and hands it to me. I smile and finger the cover longingly.

"Depends whether you like Salinger," comes her late reply.

"I do," I say. "Especially this one. It's my favorite."

She raises an eyebrow, only one, which impresses me since only my mother has mastered this skill, and says, "*Really*?" with a tone of polite disdain.

"Yes."

"It was banned, you know," she adds, thinking this will alter my opinion.

"Yes, I know," I say, with an eagerness she cannot possibly understand.

"They banned it because of the language, but I'm not so concerned about that. I'm concerned with the meaning."

"And you think there is one?" I can hear the cynicism bubbling under her surface and wish I could tell her, wish I could warn her; she is only four doors away from bitterness, and it all begins here, here with the sacrifice of meaning for something—something so much more refined.

"Yes. I think it's the story of a man, well, a boy really, trying to be a man, and how he keeps wanting to do something bad because he thinks that will make him feel more real, but he ends up doing everything good because it's in his nature—because he can't help but do what's right despite his best intentions not to. Do you see?"

She doesn't. It's a shame, I think, eyes like that and she still can't see. Eyes wide and deep in their sockets as sapphires in the mud. Blue vision narrow as a tulip stem. I wonder if I should mention Eliot instead.

"He lacks discipline," she returns. "He needs to focus. He needs to plan ahead. He needs to get a real dream instead of loafing his way through life. *He needs to work.*" Enter the bitterness. "Holden Caulfield is a lazy, self-indulgent—" then she bites her tongue and holds it tight against her teeth.

"What?" I prompt her. "A son of a bitch? What?"

"Yes," she says. "A son of a bitch. But I don't normally use words like that." I lean back in the chair, and my eyes roll back in my mind, and I almost tell her in my moment of weakness: *Oh, Linda, but you will.*

≈

At the Sears store on First Avenue, my companion in the dark coat dings the bell. As she stands to leave, and I turn my knees so she can pass, I hand her back her copy of the book. "Here," I say, but she shakes her head; she doesn't want it.

"Keep it," she says, and suddenly I am overwhelmed by a desire to pull her close to me and hug her tightly as the day she was born—or the day that I was. I want to remember her. I want to keep more than the book, more than a memory on an empty bus where we were the only riders. Maybe a curl of her hair or even a chipped fingernail or a false eyelash—anything to connect me to her and to her body, which will be mine to inhabit, mine to abandon. Someday mine to betray. But she is gone now, and I watch her walk across the gray parking lot in the fading light of day with the silver-pointed umbrella, which seems to be guiding her way. *Is it a compass or a weapon?* I wonder. Her dark coat flapping in the wind.

At this moment, omniscience is a very cruel thing—but then, perhaps, it always is. I have seen how the story begins, and I have seen how it will end: with red-throat screams and blue-flame silences and the occasional moment of joy that flickers like a sunlamp through all our gray days, beaming its promise of a false, exalted light. I know what has been and what will be, that place or point in time where the never-intended and the never-expected unite to become the Inevitable Conclusion of Our Lives. There is still time, but it is slipping, the hourglass shaken by a storm. And am I willing, with everything I know, to give it up—my single chance—my solitary privilege to be born? Am I willing to live in this world of cloistered heat and ransomed water? To watch them love uselessly, and in some hushed hours, regret even me—that thread that has woven them tight together as feathers from a fallen wing?

With my mind's eye now, I am watching. From there on the bus and deep in this dream, I look past the revolving doors of the old sagging structure—old even then in the winter of '63—and I see beyond the shallow walls to the place on the basement stairs where she will meet him; how they will both be walking in opposite directions, neither intending to stop or stay; and how she will smile shyly, reflexively, and he will stick out his hand and clasp her fingers against his cherry-young palm: both of them, un-ringed, un-weathered, loose pages still unbound. I watch him escort her to his car, late night under a voyeuristic moon, and drive her home the way he likes best—by the water—where they will stop and think of things that maybe should be said, but never are.

In fifteen years, they will imagine me; in sixteen years, I will arrive in a slippery, blood-soaked dream to consecrate their vow of almost happiness, sometimes honesty. Not quite . . . *If anyone present knows of any reason why these two should not be joined, let him speak now or forever hold his . . .* peace.

I rub my hands over the not-yet-tattered cover of J. D.'s masterpiece and turn the page. Inside is written, in certain purple ink, *Linda Smith*. It is my peace I am holding as I take this pen and scratch it out, the word—the single word—that stands between being and unborn. And with Bishop's eloquence, that is to say her strength, or selfishness, I write it *like disaster*: my own life into their story.

~~Linda Smith.~~

Linda Wade.

# Early Elegies

Back in the time when we were all unkept secrets, or stories aching to be told, I remember her. She had my mother's name, which Spanish taught me meant *beautiful* or *lovely*. Brittle bones, a childhood marred by scarlet fever, horse figurines that filled up her windowsill. Privilege, of course, is where she came from, and I can say this because I come from there, too. It's a small town just shy of the City, a frill collar decorating (perhaps disguising) the scraggly neck of some must-be-real world. But my Aunt Linda, before I knew her by that name, was a sister, somewhere back in the '60s sweater set of golden hair, glossy lips, and homespun sorority dreams.

There she is—*see her*—coming into focus on the stairs. I told you she was pretty, and I meant it, the way an archaeologist reconstructs a skeleton with skin. I see her then, walking slowly in her French-cut skirt, flounced below the waist, a belt looped loosely for effect. She takes a camel coat and camel gloves, both fur-lined for the snow chill that is Pullman. A college town, close to Idaho, where the legal drinking age is still nineteen, and she is learning how to swallow liquor quickly, without the customary wince, and how to act interested when yet another science major starts to woo.

"Linda, wait up!" I say, stepping from the shadows of the room. Her face contorts, uncomfortable, since she remembers me but can't recall my name.

"It's Julie," I offer softly, extending a burnished hand. She studies me, her own touch pale as her tone.

"Yes, that's right. I knew it was," though she blushes and quickly turns away.

Outside in the snow, our boots make deep incisions like drilling holes in teeth. She moves, as usual, with predicated grace, trailing one foot behind her in an ice-tipped arabesque. "Tell me about yourself," I say, to cut the silence. "Where did you come from? Why did you come here?"

Strangely taunted by the question, Linda looks at me, her green eyes steaming. "That's a bit austere, don't you think? I mean, this *is* 1964. There are a lot of reasons a girl comes to college these days."

"Sure there are; that's why I'm asking. What's your major and all that?" I am treading in place to keep pace with her: the slow shifts, the lean coquettish centrifuge of motion. The coyly cocking head.

"Sociology," she says, after a pause. "I'm not really sure why. I just know I like it is all, thinking about people in the larger world, and college in general, I suppose." Blushing, deep red, her cream skin mottles a rose: "And I'm sure you've noticed some awfully eligible young bachelors all around."

"Yes—and some older ones, too," thinking of the professor with whom she'll fall in love. He has my father's name—a simple one—who wouldn't trust a generous man named Bill? *William Hatch, Ph.D.*, for professional occasions: a man she'll first fall into, then fall through. But she won't meet him now, not sophomore-aged, the dilettante in cashmere and leather shoes. It will be happenstance, six years later, a sorority reunion; my dream guides us slowly through the door—familiar hallways choked with light, fragrant women posing on the stairs. Six years doesn't age a face, but darkens at the eyes: life passing: passing through, passing by.

"The workplace agrees with me," she whispers in my ear—a new Mustang, a ruby necklace, her old room still reserved in the house in Fauntlee Hills. "Mama's such a dear; I couldn't bear to leave her, especially now—now that Daddy's gone." A false security pervades her and her gestures, the smooth voice that speaks in headphones with its hushed and docile tone: "No, Mr. Connor isn't in just now; may I take a message?" And Bill is here beside the brocade curtains (someone's brother, someone's friend), taking notice, taking—what is it they say?—*a shine*. With his broad hand, he corrals her to a corner; with his wide eyes, attentive and appraising, *could she love me, could she honor and obey?*

We snap back. We return. "I'd very much like to get married," Linda says and pulls her hood up at the softest dust of snow.

≈

In the stage play, there is a curtain drawn; in the film, a lens digressed to fireworks or flowers. But in the story, as it appears on this or any page—a word, some innuendo, a swift and sweeping gaze. Linda does not stay in love. Linda does not marry. When the ring comes in its black velvet box on a little bed of satin rimmed with gold, she doesn't want it, doesn't take it, doesn't even slip it on. "Come with me," he says, his voice coercing.

"Bill," she smiles, sighs. "I've always liked that name so much. It's my brother's name, you know."

"It should be your *husband's* name. Why won't you take it?"

"You know why. I've already explained it a hundred times." She shifts, vacillates, avoiding the fastidious clasp of his eyes.

"Because I have children? Because I was married before?"

"That, and—"

"I know, I know, your mother." He heaves; keys rattle in his pocket-savvy hands. "She can move with us. There'll be plenty of room for her at the house in the Solomon Islands. The important thing is that we start our life together, and start it soon . . . . Time's ticking," he adds, trying to sound light, hopeful.

"My life is here," she tells him, "close to my family. This is where I belong. This is what I know, what I trust, . . . " mournfully trailing off.

"And what about me? I thought you trusted *me*. Not enough to actually fuck me, of course—"

"Bill!"

"—but enough to maybe, sometime after the ceremony, entertain the notion." He snaps the box shut, his large hand shaking. "You know what you are, Linda?" She doesn't look up. "You're a *fucking* Puritan. You don't want Prince Charming; you want a Quaker in a handmade carriage."

She is twenty-eight years old, a virgin: no stories yet worth saving for the dark.

≈

"Did you ever pose for pictures?" I ask. We have come in from the cold and are sitting, knees to knees, sipping coffee from chipped brown cups. Her eyebrows arch, indignant. "Not those kind of pictures," I clarify, "just pictures, prints. . . . Do you ever think about modeling?"

"No, not modeling," she sighs. "Looking good, keeping trim, those are their own rewards. A girl has to make herself appealing if she's going to find a man." Her eyes hazel, an ambiguous shade, turn suddenly, certainly green. "Are you seeing anyone?" Linda inquires.

"Seeing?" I repeat, struck by the strangeness of the phrase. *I haven't seen anyone for such a long time. It will be thirty-six years before I fall in love—the first time—forty until I find myself, a fossiled longing, preserved in my lover's eyes.* "No," I tell her quietly. "No one special. How 'bout you?"

"I go out enough," she insists. "I'm by no means the social outcast of the house," then flashes me a smile as if seeking reassurance she is right. "The fraternity boys are just so dismal sometimes, but the science types aren't much what I'm looking for at all." *Looking for.* "They're just so studious, so obsessed with their work." *Did I look for you, my love? How did I find you? Can you hear me calling through forty years of snow?* "I never really understand what they're saying."

Linda glances around the room, caressing her coffee mug. "Awfully quiet in here today, isn't it? Must be the weather. I think I'll go for a refill," she says, stretching her long legs, standing. I watch her move away, slowly as always, sleek wool of her skirt cresting over her skin in pleated and uniform waves. *This is how I will begin to envy; this is how I will learn what beauty is—a body—lithe and lean, lacking in imperfection—skin so white and so clean.* I watch her at the counter, leaning, bending in her willowy way, filling the cup that will never run over, that will continue to slip away. And I see her, ten and fifteen years into the future, her shoulders stooped, her spine piercing its residual pain. She fills her cup, monogrammed in yellow cursive *Linda Ann, Linda Ann,* and her fingers shake as she takes up the phone: "No, Mr. Connor isn't in just now; may I take a message?" There are years coming, steep as a ladder built from stones, a staircase perpetually ascending. And she rises early and earlier, consumes her seventh cup while waiting for the bus. I see her, ten and fifteen cups into the morning, trembling, tearful, the decade's headache she just can't seem to cure.

I snap back. I return. Her pockets empty, she pours the last of her coins down the silver throat of the jukebox, its song welling up, softly at first, then slowly gathering steam. "It's 'King of the Road,'" she says beaming, bending over the table, sliding into her chair. I study her features—delicate, small—while she prattles on: "Roger Miller is an awfully good singer, I think. I know some people wouldn't agree. . . ." I am surprised, then saddened: *one day I will starve myself so I can look exactly like this—the dainty hairpins, the elegant flip, the sepia face in the photograph with its still-ungratified wish.* She sips her coffee with sugar and cream. I gaze under her skin to her bones.

$$\approx$$

The sky is purple and swollen with snow. A superficial darkness falls. "It never gets this cold in Seattle," she says, and I nod my head to agree. "Do you know Seattle?" she asks suddenly. "It just occurred to me; I've never asked you where you're from."

"Yes," I say, "I've lived in Seattle my whole life," my life that has yet to begin. "I'm from the West side, near the ferry docks in Fauntleroy."

"Really? That's funny," she says. "I thought I knew everyone there." I shrug, trudge on through the bruised light, listening as the tree boughs snap under their burdens. "Did you always know you wanted to be an Alpha Phi?"

"A what?" I tend to forget the name of her sorority house, though its folk-lore in our family will abound.

"An Alpha Phi, silly!" she chides, kicking the snow gingerly in my direction.

"Oh, no, not really. I didn't plan on coming here at all."

"Yes, I know what you mean," she says, "but with all the women at college these days, what a shame it would be if we didn't unite. . . . I've never had a blood sister," she sighs, "but a sorority sister seems almost as good."

We reach the house: a fire flaming in the stone hearth, a few fragrant girls in the hall. "Would you like to see my room?" Linda offers with a hopeful smile. "I keep some things there I don't show many folks, but after all, you're a West Seattle girl and one of my very own sisters."

"Yes, all right," as I follow her up the stairs.

"Dale thinks they gave me the best room," she grins. "It's a little smaller than some of the other ones, but I share it with only one other girl." The door creaks, swings open. We step into her hallowed space, and Linda reaches for the lamp—rip cord she pulls in the dark. My squinting eyes suddenly flood.

"Did you paint these, Linda?" knowing she did, knowing they will cover my grandmother's walls as Band-Aids disguise broken skin.

"Yes," proudly and shyly at the same time. She shows me her sketchbook, her collection of paints, and explains how she sits up late on the window ledge, drinking coffee and drawing pictures of horses and flowers.

"Why horses and flowers?" I ask, something I've always wondered.

"Well, because they're beautiful, and because they're free. There's nothing more beautiful and free in the whole world than a horse or a flower."

Nodding, I bow my head as in prayer. "Do you want to do something with these pictures? Do you want to show them somewhere?" My heart is heavy with elegy; the words come softly, more somber than I could intend.

She fondles one of the frames: sloppy green paint borders a dark-gray gelding at play. "No, no, nothing like that. It's just a hobby, something to do, something to pass the time." She stands by the window, a gold silhouette—a birch tree, ever so gently, bent. "And once you're married with children and all, there's no time for hobbies like this."

Christmas is coming. Here in the Other Time on the other side of the mountains, Linda offers me a ride home. *Home, where is home? I hear you wondering, forty years ahead of me inside the future.* I accept because I am weary, because I am stranded here, small coin stuffed in a pocket. I think of you, your body beside me in a distant bed. *Wake me!* I can feel my mouth calling. I already know how this story ends.

"It's the least I can do," Linda murmurs. "After all, we are from the same part of town." She carries her suitcase, canvas and white, a clutch purse tucked under her arm. "Now you mustn't mind Daddy; he always makes jokes. He's just the most horrible tease." I move slowly this time, dragging my empty bag.

"Yes, I was going to ask you about your parents. Are you sure I haven't imposed?"

"No, don't be silly! They were only too eager to please. My brother would be coming with them," she sighs, "but apparently he has a new squeeze."

"Oh." Then, cautiously: "Haven't you met her yet?"

"No, probably over Christmas, though. Her name is Linda, I know that much, and Mama says she thinks it's serious." Linda shrugs and straightens her hat, a side-tipped, red-wool beret. "It's only been a couple of months. I doubt it's *that* serious."

What she doesn't know is how she will grow to loathe my mother, how they will snipe at each other over sweet rolls and copious Caesar salads. I see them now as always, fingers crooked and pointing, Linda Ann Wade and Linda Marie. She turns to me, leans close till her mouth nearly touches my ear: "It's sad to say, but my brother has awfully poor taste in women."

Down the gravel road a wine-colored Mercury rambles. Headlights switch off; a door winces open; two figures emerge from the car.

"Mama! Daddy!" Linda falls into her mother's arms.

"Oh, darling, how we've missed you!" her mother's low gracious voice unfolds. I hang back, staring. I can't stop myself. I won't see her again till she's old.

"Julie, I want you to meet my mother. Mama, this is my friend Julie from school."

"Very pleased to meet you, Julie. I'm June," my someday-grandmother says.

*Yes, it's me! I'm Bill's daughter! Can't you see it? Please recognize me.*

But she doesn't. She smiles. Her teeth are shiny and white; the gold ones have yet to appear. "My," she says, "you're such a tall girl. And we thought our Linda was tall."

I study her features. She is sturdy and straight; she is not slumped yet, not shrunken with widowhood and an ever-declining weight. Her fingers extend—tapered, un-palsied—and I touch her, disbelieving: the arthritis absent, the anguish absent, the abundance of dark brown hair.

"Oh, please, where are my manners? Julie, let me introduce my husband, John."

My grandfather, whose face is reserved for the safety of photographs, steps forward. He has been loading the car with our luggage; he has been shivering and warming his hands with the weakening breath of his lungs. "Julie," he says, "it's a pleasure." There are the keen eyes, the salesman's smile, the cautiously clefted chin. I am inventorying him, and he senses it—he, of all people, the one I have never met. He, of all of them, understands best; he in his waning days, his last slow and surreptitious hours. We are passing each other, he into darkness and I into light, discovering here at this juncture that they are perhaps the same place.

"So, you're a West Seattle girl," he says, with a voice eerily reminiscent of my father's. Always talking, always gentle and jolly in his scripted salesman's way. "Tell us about yourself. What's your family name? Where are they from?"

Sliding into the backseat, I stare forward, meeting his eyes in the mirror. "Julie's always so reluctant to talk about herself," Linda exclaims, resting her hand on my knee.

"Go ahead, dear, don't be shy," my grandmother says. She is applying her lipstick in the passenger mirror but turns to flash me a smile.

"Well, my father was born in Montana."

"June, did you hear that? They're from Montana as well."

"I heard, John dear, but please keep your eyes on the road."

"Were you born in Montana then?" Linda inquires.

"No—I mean, well, actually, *yes*," I lie, suddenly panicked, recalling the date and time.

And the family, so familiar with Montana, still longing for its summer heat, its flat and winding roads, usurps the story that is not mine to tell, their voices crowding each other in pleasant cacophony: *Linda was only eight when we left, she hardly remembers that winters in Billings were so much colder than this . . . better jobs out West, you know, I work for Goodyear . . . Seattle is really a lovely place to raise a family . . . I'm used to the water now; I would miss it if it weren't there. . . .*

"I wish you could meet our son, Bill, but he's always so busy working." It is my grandfather speaking, his eyes trained on mine through the mirror.

I choke a little. "What does he do?"

"Oh, what doesn't he do?" my grandmother intercedes. "That boy is working all the time, going to school at the University, rowing on the—what do they call that again, Johnny?"

"The crew team, dear."

"Yes, that's right, he does his crew and his studies and that young manager's training program at Sears. Truly, we hardly see him at all these days, and he lives in our very same city! And then Linda goes off to college all the way over in Pullman. I can't wait till it's finished, and you can move back to us, dear."

"I know, Mama, I know. We've been over this all before. I wanted to go someplace different, to see what it was like. Just for a little while. Julie understands, don't you?" Her eyes coax me to assure her of some small degree of autonomy.

"I think it's good to get away," I say, thinking of my own mother who will scream and sob, shattering the glasses in her kitchen. *Don't leave me! You're my whole life! I have nothing else to live for without you!*

"Oh, I know it's a good experience, and there might even be an MRS degree in it for you girls," my grandmother smiles.

They are all smiles, creased and pressed, with features that blur into the deep furrow of conformity, of acquiescence.

"I'm not sure I'll marry," I say— just to say it, just to hear myself forecast the future aloud.

"Oh, nonsense, you're a lovely girl. It just takes patience is all. Johnny and I didn't marry until I was twenty-eight years old. I was quite the old maid for my time!"

"Don't listen to her," John tells me, winking in the mirror. It has become our private portal of communication. "She was beautiful, the best-looking clerk of the bunch."

"He used to come to the store where I worked. I sold jewelry, and he bought my own engagement ring from me—can you imagine?"

"—Three weeks after I met her! She thought it was for another girl!"

"Six months later we were married, and the rest is history," my young grandmother proclaims with a flourish. "But I was prepared for the worst, you know. I went to night school, and I got my degree. I knew if I didn't meet a good man, I wasn't going to settle for anyone less, and that's why I've always encouraged Linda to go to school and at least learn to do office work in case her Prince Charming is, well, *unavoidably detained*."

I watch as Linda smiles, her complexion suddenly carnationed. She doesn't suspect, doesn't imagine that her body will be empty of lovers and children, that her breasts—untouched and untested—will hoard a dark secret, the tumor growing smugly inside the loosening flesh, greedily feeding on skin, her blood-shot and withering nipple. She will crumple like a wilted corsage on a teenager's bedside table—the prom over, the dancing never begun—and her old mother, ninety-one, hunched over a cane, will tend her indefinitely.

They cannot imagine, and I grant them their peace, temporal though it will be. I allow them to love earnestly, each one and another, before the malignancy.

"What is it you plan to do, dear?" My grandmother is looking at me.

"Me? I'm—" I catch my grandfather's eye. "—I'm a writer, actually, or at least I want to be."

"A writer? Well, that's wonderful! John, did you hear that? Linda's something of a writer, too."

"Is she?"

"No, not really, I just dabble," she says. "I write poems sometimes, just for something to do." I know already, but I am interested in spite of myself, and her mother urges her to recite. "They're not very long," Linda begins apologetically. "Usually I don't even write them down."

"Go ahead, dear. The one you wrote for Easter service."

"OK." She pauses and wets her painted lips. "The beauty of this world is God's, the ugliness is man's. I hate to see a God-made world destroyed by human hands." I am saying it with her. In my head, I hear the words hovering over my plate, another grace pronounced at our common table.

Her father takes his hands off the steering wheel long enough to proudly applaud. "We have a poet in the family," he smiles.

And my grandmother, tersely—"John, watch the road!"

≈

When we arrive in Fauntleroy, I feel the landscape shifting, rising under the wheels studded for adverse conditions. My grandfather covers seven states; he drives for hours in the snowy dark. "But here," he grins, "everything's mild. No big blizzards. Nothing to worry about."

"You can let me off here," I say, pointing to the ferry dock and the waiting cars like a row of beads.

"But what about your house? Your family?" my driver protests. "We'd be happy to take you right to your door."

I smile now, stepping out into the sea-thick air, the seagulls cawing above. "There isn't a door. It hasn't been built yet," I say, and their faces gleam back through the glass. "None of it's happened. All of it will. I thank you, though, for the ride."

My grandfather, whom I will not see again in life or elsewhere, opens the trunk and hands me my unneeded bag. "Are you sure you'll be all right?" he asks, looking around, puzzled but not quite concerned.

"Yes, thank you," I say.

"Have a good day!" Linda waves from the car. "I'll see you after the holidays!"

I turn back to the beach, to the logs belted with kelp and donning their seaweedy gowns. There is a woman there, bending down. I recognize her as the one who will wake me forty years from now in the warm bed of the future. But I turn back again, once more, to the old Mercury sailing away. I wave to them— my future family, my already history.

I say it, trembling and a little too soft: "Have a beautiful rest of your days."

# Third Door

In the studio—soft blur of lights, distant hum, rows of blue-vinyl seats with shiny armrests. At the helm—velvet curtains and a glittering marquee; footstep directives from Stage Left and Stage Right down the side aisles and up to the balcony. These names in lights: *$64,000 Question*, *I've Got a Secret*, *Queen for a Day*, *The Price Is Right*, *To Tell the Truth*, and *This Is Your Life*. Today's date is January 14, 1961—I read it in the log—and the only contestant slated to appear is a seventeen-year-old high school senior from Seattle. Her name is Linda Smith. Her vital statistics are as follows:

*She's a reserved young lady with exceptional manners. Oldest of three children. Determined to put away a little money for college. She's had some hard times: father's been out of work off and on; mother makes most of her clothes. Nothing if not ambitious. Found her first job as seasonal help at the Sears, Roebuck & Company; intends to stay on if they'll have her. Special talents include playing accordion in the school marching band, a passionate love of music (particularly old songs), and a reasonable singing voice. Wants to be a schoolteacher and likes to study French. Has a gift for the acquisition of languages.*

It doesn't matter that I don't exist yet: chronology a cocoon that has to get shed if any future is fated to emerge. Or any past—for that is what this is—to surface in the scuffed and cryptic crystal ball. I walk behind the turnstiles and the three revolving doors. I find the pendulum platforms where each of the prizes is stored. And not just stored—*arranged*. The well-choreographed design sets of these lives. Parentheses couching words like (Possible) and (Maybe). A recliner tipped back with the weight of (Most Likely). Ottoman for an unwitting actor to trip over in a future part: still shrink-wrapped with the manufacturer's warning: (Default) (Proxy).

Behind Door #1, I find my father. He is twenty years old and dressed in his wedding tuxedo. I drink him in: tall glass of water in the stuffy heat of the stage. He paces back and forth in his new black shoes with the tassels, then sits down and spontaneously spit-shines them. "You can tell a good man by his shoes," Bill says, not the least surprised to see me standing there. "By his handshake and the shine of his shoes. Gotta be firm. Gotta be polished." I nod. I am mouthing along.

"So, when is the wedding?" I ask, gesturing to his boutonniere, still preserved in its plastic casement—the seal intact like a contract yet to be signed.

"I'm early," he says. "Not for five years. But you know what they say: it's the early bird who gets the worm."

"And you feel pretty sure she'll choose you?"

His brow furrows, fixity suddenly marred. "How could she not? I've done some research. Did you know that 90 percent of contestants ultimately select the first door?" He stands again, stretches his long legs with the black satin pinstripes down the sides. "And when she's ready for me, I'll be waiting. I'll probably be running my own Sears store by then. I've got my eyes keen on the one in Ballard."

"Tell the truth," I command him. We will never be this candid again. "What is it you want from your life?"

"Is this for the big prize?"

"The biggest."

"You mean, the $64,000?"

"I mean everything."

"To do the right thing, of course"—and I am touched by his raw sincerity, his belief in fantastical odds. Still, I must test him.

"Is there only one right thing, Bill?" I try to make a joke, even though it's his life—and mine—we're talking about. After all, for every diagnosis there's a second opinion. Sometimes even a third.

He considers it a moment, then me; then a cloud comes over his eyes. "Are you sure you work here?" Suddenly suspicious: "Where is your clipboard?"

"I left it in my office," I say. "But I'm comfortable working from memory, if you are."

He nods, soberly now, and resolves: "There's only one right thing for me, and it's the same right thing for Linda. We're going to have a wonderful life."

"Do you want my advice? I've worked in theater a long time. I'm a consummate actor, a pro."

"But—" bewildered—"this is a game show."

The hum in my head growing stronger, surpassing the lights: "*This is your life.*"

He nods again, smiling this time. "*Exactly.*"

≈

"We're on in five, four, three—"

They are all here: Hal March, Garry Moore, Jack Bailey, and Ralph Edwards: a row of stalwart men in charismatic formation, checker-print jackets, and ever-widening ties. Here before my eyes they stand in color—each bearing a slender microphone (a single sterling rose) and clapping along with the crowd. The Master of Ceremonies behind them, descending the stand-alone stairs. "Bill Cullen!" the announcer decrees, but I gasp as I recognize my grandfather, their resemblance in retrospect often remarked. And it might be said of John Campbell Wade as it was said of Bill Cullen: "No scandal has ever been associated with this man."

"Greetings to all of you in our studio audience!" He turns to me, slightly left of center, recoiling from the spotlight's gleam. We contemplate each other briefly before he pivots to the camera and declares: "Welcome to Culver City's Best Night of Television! Games, Games, and More Games!"

His body itself an exclamation mark: broad shoulders tapering to the points of his bright tasseled shoes, the loud yellow jacket, the throaty smoker's voice. . . . "Stay tuned for excitement, ladies and gentlemen, boys and girls—"

I am paralyzed, here in this ellipsis of eternal moments. Eyelids heavy but unbearably open. *Propped.* I clutch this curtain, as though it were a gown.

All eyes attend my young mother as she steps up to the podium. She wears false eyelashes and a lavish wig, and from this angle, I can see that she is shaking. She has high cheekbones and stunning blue eyes—

The draperies swing open at the back of the stage, revealing a projection screen. As the screen descends and the lights dim and the music swells, sudden and symphonic—her body shifts, her centerpiece glides to the side.

"This is your life!" the Bill Cullen impersonator cries. Grainy surface of sixteen millimeters; sepia square positioned at the precise radial point of nowhere. My mother's story, edited for television and recast with old-time movie flair.

Victor Borge might accompany on piano, with intermittent comic routine. I half expect Lawrence Welk and his orchestra to release a trumpet's worth of bubbles into the air. *Champagne music.* And what are we to celebrate? The inevitability of it all, the phantom choices? She looks less cynical now, holding her hands in patient posture as if anticipating prayer. I hold back the barking dogs of my heart, leash them tight.

*Let her live a while longer,* I instruct myself. *When you wake up, it all comes down. Avalanche of confetti, curls.* Receding further into the shadows, bowing my head. *The avalanche, and then the final curtain.*

I see the public swimming pool, children skirting its ledges and stairs. I watch them shivering in the cool breeze of the Northwest summer, their mothers clenching them in tight jaws of towels. And Linda. And Sharon—little sister tagging along. They are walking through the woods, Lincoln Park in late afternoon, Sharon teasing and Linda looking ever straighter ahead, eyes narrowing toward a perceptible part in the trees. White sky like the scalp behind it.

"What would you do if I ran away from you right now? What would you do if I disappeared, and you couldn't find me?"

"I could always find you," Linda insists, her hold on her sister's wrist slackening, as if to dare.

"How do you know?"

"Because I've been exploring these woods longer than you have, and because Mother trusts me, and I'm not going to let her down."

"Stephanie from school has a house by the water. What if we went over there for dinner? They usually have a barbecue."

"You know the rules: to the pool and home again. Checkpoints. No dilly-dallying."

"We wouldn't have to stay long—at Stephanie's house." Linda looks down, lips poised to chide her sister, and a twig snaps. Eerie how the bright screen magnifies the sound. How the sound turns metonymous, standing in for a whole range of sounds, sensations, textures. Somewhere in the cinematic distance, a horseshoe toss gone bad: clanking, cursing. My own story caught in that caesura, suspended between a snap and a sigh.

The man does not require a name. No credit will be given him when the credits roll. This archetypal Stranger, roaming the woods, playing on the cultivated fears of children. Linda will remember him; Sharon will not—their collective truth a split still, a double negative.

"We don't want your candy!" the younger declares, her light curls shaking their renunciation.

"Well, that's good then. I don't think I have any candy."

In profile now: khaki trenchcoat, furtive eyes. "Would you like to check my pockets just in case?"

Linda's wan face puckering, approximating courage. "Leave us alone. Step out of the way."

"Gladly," he says. "It wasn't my intention to intimidate you." Stepping aside, the Stranger opens his coat, nude body hairy and hunkering. Sharon pulls free from Linda's clasp, stubby legs churning fast and not looking back—all the way down to the water. Her sister transfixed, the body terrifying and luminous in a spotlight of sun. They stand there, tense, fingers loose at their sides as if considering which guns to draw, which imaginary weapons. My mother, at twelve, stiff as a mannequin, fixed and unflinching. A look in her eyes that I recognize: not a white flag in sight, not a whiff of the scent of surrender.

≈

The stage switches to chaos at the onslaught of Commercial Break. Kaleidoscope of kitsch and conversation. I wander back behind the tall metal rods and orange traffic cones, ropes for changing backdrop boards and sliding curtains. Door #2 is a dressing room, and I knock tentatively, my anonymous fist blank and white at the knuckles. Numb.

"Come in," a woman's lilting voice replies.

And there in the swivel chair teasing her dark mountain of extravagant hair is JoAnne Brower, who went by another name back then, though I can't quite recall it. *Before she married Hal,* my mother said, *she was the most boy-crazy girl you ever met. Your father and I used to marvel that she ever settled down.*

"How do I look, darling?" asks JoAnne, extending her ivory-smooth and unadorned hands. I move toward her as if we are going to spin circles together like ring-around-the-rosy on an autumn afternoon under the most exceptional oak tree in all of Hiawatha Park. We have done this before. I remember how she told me she loved to be dizzy, and we laid in the leaves and laughed and laughed when my mother came and claimed she couldn't find us.

"I just bought this fabric at Jo-Ann's," she says, caressing the gauzy blouse that curves around her generous bosom. "I have to shop there—on principle, you know. Sometimes I have them page me in the store, so I can pretend I'm the Jo-Ann who owns it!"

Yes, I remember her now: the wild green eyes, the dazzling smile. "My father used to say you were a live wire."

"Your father, eh? Did I sleep with him too in my Catholic school days?" And she laughs and slips her arm through my hips like a sash.

"I've missed you, JoAnne," I say suddenly.

"Well, I'll be! People missing me all over the place, and sweetheart, I didn't even know we had met." She poses on the powder-blue sofa, patting the seat beside. "Would you be a doll and zip me up?"

Yes, I remember her now: the dark moles on her back she didn't want to remove; *how would I look in my bathing suit?* And when they turned, amorphous, with the skin peeling back, and her doctor pronounced the dreaded double syllable, she shrugged it all off like an unneeded shawl, the slightest wince in her sigh: "Cancer is my birth sign, you know. The Big Crab. We're cranky in the mornings and tough as all hell. I have a shell that concrete couldn't crack." My mother's best friend since junior high school, with the unkempt curls, the car that stalled at every intersection.

"So, let's get down to the dirty talk. Any good-looking bachelors out there?"

"I thought you were married," I say.

"Me? Oh, hell no, honey! I'm not the marrying kind. My girls and I have the very best time. . . . "

Thinking of her son Chris, my friend and fellow only child: "You have daughters now?"

"*Kids*? Are you crazy? It's my *girls* I'm talking about, my *women*—they'd be like my sorority sisters if any of us had been fool enough to join." I must look startled or sad, for she taps my wrist and whispers—"Hey, you're not in a sorority, are you?"

"No," shaking my head and beginning to smile. "No, no, not even close."

"Well, good, because as far as I'm concerned, they're a blazing trail of bitches, the whole lot of them. I've got Wanda and Nancy watching my back, and the queen of them all, my Linda."

An image sweeps through me like a seasonal wind: *her Linda*, who is also my own, stooping on the broad cathedral stairs. Almost statuesque in the autumn light, this woman who claimed she "couldn't stand Catholics."

*But your best friend!* I protest.

*She was different.*

Holy Rosary at midday: the church bells toll. I watch the funeral pass by my fifth-grade window.

"Linda Smith and JoAnne Kearney, living the high life, traveling all over the place. Forget all your worries, forget all your cares; teachers by day and rebels by night!" She raises an imaginary glass and toasts it with mine; we sit a long time together, quietly sipping.

Yes, I remember her now: the Rhoda friend, with the gold hoop earrings and the incense sticks . . . the Catholic hippie boy-crazy lady . . . *champagne music!*

≈

"Are you trying out for *Queen for a Day*?"

*It's her, it's Linda, the only one I'm certain will see through me. She was always more suspicious than other people. And now my cover's blown. What to say?*

Here we are, face to face behind the shifting scenes—my mother the funhouse mirror in which I find myself: each knot and crevice, cramp and slant, collage of selves sewn on like buttons. Every wrinkle of her broomstick skirt, every blotted lipstick tissue and perspiration stain. Loitering like lint, exhibitioning like slip: treacherous proximity: the two of us nearly close enough to merge.

I shake my head, blushing.

"I heard about one woman whose house got damaged in a mudslide. They gave her all new furniture *and* a Hawaiian vacation."

"Wow," I say, still expecting her intuitive interception. But when it doesn't come, I press her: "So, what is it you hope to win?"

"Well, I've always dreamed I'd be the choice contestant on a show like *The Price Is Right*. People are drawn at random, I think. You have to be really lucky."

"Are you?"

Now it's her turn. She shakes her head, white skin mottling red: "Not really. At least I haven't been so far. Luck can change, I'm sure, but if you want something bad enough, I think you have to *make* it happen. It's not just if the shoe fits; it's not just fate."

Nodding now, implicitly: "What makes Cinderella so goddamn special? That the idea? Why shouldn't we all be queen for a day?"

She eyes me apprehensively as a slow seam unravels: "You remind me of someone."

Eagerly: "Who?"

"A friend of mine. She says witty things like you. When we go to the movies, she always talks back."

And coincidentally, here we are at the movies.

I ask Linda if she would like to accompany me to the green room. "We can see everything from there," I promise. "It's a kind of privileged view."

Hesitating: "I'd like to but—don't I have to stay here? Isn't there something in my contract?"

"Don't worry," I assure her, placing a provisional hand on her padded shoulder. "I know this place inside and out. I have connections."

≈

The screen again: sepia square enlarging to the margins. *Cinéma vérité* to the third power raised: she smiles as I say it, likes the sound. "It's French," she volunteers, looking up from the couch in a childlike way, coquettishly seeking to impress me.

"It's also a filming style." In my element now, relaxing: "It's known for combining naturalistic techniques from documentary work with the storytelling typical of a scripted film." My hypothetical mother younger than I—self-conscious, voracious, a teacher-to-be.

"It literally means *film truth*."

Assembling a puzzle together, as we will do at the dining room table a double decade from now: beginning with the borders, then conscientiously filling in until every last piece has found its place inside the portrait.

"You're smart," she observes. "I guess you must have studied a lot in college."

Our eyes meeting, holding; still, she doesn't recognize: *please, Mom, please, you know me, you want to know me* . . . and once again, the thick brocade curtains start to rise.

≈

That "grand undefined term," that *mise-en-scène*: this time we land inside a bowling alley. There is Linda, aged sixteen, gauntly thin and artificial in her movements.

"You look like a marionette," I tell her, emboldened by the dark. "So phony I can almost see your strings."

Not the defensiveness I expect, or the anger: "It's over," she relents. "I'm doing better now. I owe a lot of it to my friendship with Bill Pommer."

Like a cue in a stage play, he emerges on screen, bald at sixteen with a stocky awkward figure. "Do you want me to show you again?" he asks. "There's a science to this, if you'd care to be precise about it."

They stand close to the red line, borderland between their common space and the solitary sanctity of a long gleaming lane. They know better than to let their feet cross over. Instead, she bends down, and he stretches her arm back gracefully, the bare goose-bumped skin and her sleeveless turtleneck sweater. "That's it, reaching all the way back, as far as your body will let you. None of this squatting with your bum in the air and rolling the ball with both hands. You can do better than that. You're a natural."

And when she releases the ball, wavering in its trajectory toward the ten attentive pins, their bodies crouch together, as close as they can get without stepping over. She grabs his hand, braces herself from toppling. But in the end, it's a split, the most difficult kind—with only the 7 and 10 pins left standing.

"It looks like someone's mouth with all the front teeth missing," Linda sighs. "Let's do something else, Bill. Teach me to drive."

As she turns to face him, their bodies collide. His hands tremble to her shoulders but will not retract. He kisses her full on the mouth, hard and fast as if rehearsing a scene he is terrified at once to play and not to play. Overqualified for the role, there is no telling how long he has waited. Bill stuffs his hands deep in his corduroy pockets, fidgets. "*Carpe diem.* It's Latin," he says, with a shy kind of pride. "It's a credo of mine—*seize the day.*"

"Bill, you know you're one of my best friends, don't you? The very best if you don't count JoAnne."

"I know."

"But if you go around kissing me like that, people are liable to think we're more than friends, and we might get confused ourselves."

"I know."

"We don't want to tie ourselves down now, do we? I mean, in a couple of years, you'll go off to seminary, and I'll get my teaching degree, and—there's just no telling."

"I know."

He doesn't look at her, and she shifts uneasily in her blue jeans with gold seams and cuffs rolled up above her ankles.

It is the oldest story the cinema cares to recount: the Plight of the Unrequited. He loves her, but she doesn't love him. They stay friends; he takes fishing trips with her future husband. She isn't happy, and neither is he, but the math involved exceeds simple principles of addition and subtraction. She will never love him, and he will always love her: binaries hardening, polarities intact. Two marriages and a bankruptcy later, he still protests—*If Linda had loved me, things would be different.*

Unlacing her shoes now, grinning up at him: that casualness only youth can afford: "Come on, Bill, teach me to drive."

≈

"Tell me why you didn't want Bill Pommer. He seemed to care so much. You seemed to trust him more than almost anyone else."

She is honest now, uncompromising—more than I could have hoped for, yet harder somehow to hear: "He's not going anywhere. Bill is . . . well, he's a dreamer. I respect him and all, and everybody knows ministers are good people, but he's never going to make a lot of money."

"How do you know?"

"I can tell. He's not that ambitious. He'll probably end up a youth minister or working for a church in some *unpaid capacity*. He just wants to have fun all the time."

"Is that so bad?"

"No. Not *bad*," Linda sighs. "He's a great friend. He's just not dating material."

"Who would be—dating material, I mean?"

She stretches her legs and moves around the room, eyes riveted always to the screen. "He'd have to be accomplished. He'd have to bring home good money or, at the very least, have the *potential* to bring home good money. And he'd have to be tall and have a full head of hair." She tightens her hands, a twisted knot of resolve. "I'd rather be single my whole life than be seen with a man who didn't look right."

≈

Having finished her first two rounds of competition, Linda Smith is led away to an isolation booth. There, in the translucent cube, in front of countless, scrupulous witnesses, she will listen to voices piped in through a PA system. Some from her future, some from her past; she must identify correctly as many as she can.

I am backstage again, having nowhere to be and passing unnoticed among members of the perfunctory crew. Door #3. A trap door in the heavy planked boards of the floor. Dingy from disuse. Rusted handle and protruding nails. *Dare I descend? Will anyone attempt to intercept me?*

The small wooden stairs quaver beneath the weight of my body. The stench of mildew is strong, like the hold of a ship packed tight with perishable goods. I almost turn back, but there's a word I love, in my real life of old books and warm blankets and one particularly beautiful girl. I wrap it around my waist like a lasso. *Scopophilia.* Let me down gently into this dark. Let me rejoice a while longer in this love of looking.

One handheld video camera. Crates and boxes, enough for a makeshift chair. (Default.) (Proxy.) I sit down. I put my eye close to the lens, like the doctor's machine and the puff of air: preparing—as if for an optical exam. I expect the letters and pointing which way the "E" is facing, and when I can see it better and when worse and when I can't see it at all anymore. But instead, the dizzy screen settles over two faces, a close-up of two pretty girls. Documented in the left-hand corner: *7.3.61. Take 1. True Stories.*

One is my mother at seventeen, a month after graduating high school. The other is a figure I don't recognize, features unfamiliar but admirable. This is the balcony of the Lewis and Clark Theater in Tukwila, Washington. I have been there before. It is still standing. They sit alone at the mezzanine level, Linda and the anonymous girl. They are whispering and sharing popcorn, and their bare legs in the sticky heat are touching. Is there a word for this—watching someone who is watching someone else?

"Lara, I don't know what's going on."

"So pay better attention." Her scolding tone soon transforms into smile.

"What's it supposed to be about again? And why is it called *The Misfits*?"

"It's from the play—by Arthur Miller. Shut up and watch. It's perfect. *She's* perfect."

But Linda is pestering again, leaning in close until her hair brushes against Lara's angular, slightly anguished face. "Who's perfect?"

"*Marilyn.* She's a goddess. She's like the best-looking woman alive. And not just alive now. I think she's the best-looking woman who maybe ever lived."

Lara's dark eyes flicker; her hands clasp the armrests tightly. She is holding on, as if for dear life. Linda kisses her, softly, on the cheek.

"What did you do that for?"

"I don't know."

Lara regards her in refracted screen glow, glossy and flattering against a backdrop of torpid shadows. "I try not to think about it," she murmurs.

"What?"

"With you. Just with you. You're so—I don't know—*innocent.*"

Linda, shaking her head in protest: "I'm not innocent. I promise I'm not."

"But that's exactly the kind of thing an innocent person says. *I promise I'm not.*" Lara touches her face now, the line of her neck to the place where her white collar opens. "It's not that I don't—it's that I do—too much. You're different. It would have to be different with you."

"Lara, I don't know what you're saying. I don't understand."

Turning back to the film, voice faint as fade-out: "I've been here before. It's hard to shake. If you open that door, I'm not sure you can go back again. . . . I'm not sure you can close it."

"Why don't you kiss me?" Linda's voice—husky; her body—pent.

The scene is nearly too much for me: too sensate, profuse. Yet it is always, also, never enough.

*This invisible fist*, I tell you. *This fourth wall.*

"I can't." Lara's tears little specks on her face, sparkling.

But then she kisses her, despite her best intention not to, and the popcorn spills—confetti across their knees, petals nestling in skirt pleats. Tongues, hands, hair entangled. The decadence of first lusts, doubly forbidden: a primrose torpedo to the heart. "That grand undefined term," that *mise-en-scène*.

*Call it kismet*, my father once said. *That thing that's meant to happen, that you can't deny.*

≈

What's wrong with me that I need this—the scene set, the possibility en-acted? Is it gratuitous? Compulsive? What would the Shrink say, the Stranger? My young mother, before she belonged to anyone—no boughs bent, no cradles fallen—might have known what I know, might have felt it careening through her veins like a car on a cliffside road. That spectacular, spectatorial proposi-tion. What is her white blouse but a white flag? What can she do—here in this ellipsis space, this parenthetical—but let her buttons slip off in surrender?

≈

My mother has already chosen my father: that faithful first door. Orion, old glittering standard. One of the most recognizable patterns of stars in the northern sky, best seen in January. All these bright nebula we still believe in, stake our lives on, accept against fantastical odds.

The past will be rewritten, the future carefully contrived, and when I look for the distant lights flashing, they will turn protective, coy: *What an imagina-tion! Tell the truth. Come now, we were never On the Air.*

My father, perched on an ottoman in the faux living room. *Happenstance* conjunction of *happiness* and *chance*. He'll take his chances. He always has. It's really so simple. In the end, it's all about math: men and women, two by two: the Ark exemplar, two yields three on up to infinity. Footstep directives. Exponen-tial marquees. My voice in his ear, and his father's: hot breath blowing in har-mony: *Gotta be firm. Gotta be polished. Do the right thing, Bill. This is your life. Exactly.*

III

# A Life under Water

*This is the place.*
*And I am here, the mermaid whose dark hair*
*streams black, the merman in his armored body.*
—Adrienne Rich

The sea has always come naturally to me. I am a native speaker of wave, a nubile swimmer at ease in the surf, a lover of starfish and salt. It's true you can't step twice in the same river, but the ocean is always the same: its lusty recursive circles, its breathless eternal allure.

Most of what I know comes back to me now in tide pools, small inlets between mossy stones where understanding ebbs and settles. Like the first time my father told me sand was made of glass. I looked around us, up and down the shore, at families flying kites and spreading checkered picnic cloths, and suddenly how precious we all seemed, there among those shards disguised as grains. I marveled also at our resilience: elasticity of skin, the good heat drying us clean to our salty rims, the shifting line between land and tide and how we could cross it again and again, versatile as molecules in their changing states of matter: the liquid and solid in each of us, our effortless fluctuations.

It was my grandmother who confided "the moon controls the tides," and I thought of tugboats, tiny by comparison, guiding the massive weight of freighters. This moon, so small sometimes as to disappear all together—into its own sea of clouds or cloaks of darkness. Even then, how it was tethered to the oscillating earth, lunar strings cinching the ocean's girth and drawing it forward, then tugging it—forcefully, faithfully—back.

My grandfather, who died before my time, believed the ocean could cure us of all ills. Dead at sixty, the great irony was that he drowned in his hospital bed, each lung filled to brimming then spilling, the quiet capsize of his otherwise indestructible body. But I'm told that in his day Grandpa John was a regular Ponce de León, claiming the ocean itself as his Fountain of Youth, puffing with pride as he proclaimed: "Forget oracles. Forget shrines. Go head to toe into that wild spume; it'll batter your worst right out of you!"

At age four, my parents took me on a pilgrimage, our first journey south to Seaside, Oregon. I had seen the Bay, had seen the Sound. I woke mornings to the seagulls' caw, the salt-tinged whiff of the rain. But I had yet to fix my eyes on the Ocean: this Promised Land-not-land my father loved beyond reason. Perhaps my mother stayed in our hotel room. Perhaps she wandered the length of the promenade. I lose track of her, in my memory, where moments at the sea are concerned. It was my father who ran with me, following the low guttural moan, the steady reverberation of wave upon wave until we crossed over the boardwalk and sunk down into the sand; I kept running, all the way to the water's edge, sensing it was dangerous and miraculous both at once and feeling I must take some part in it, no matter what the cost.

This is the baptism I remember: full and vigorous immersion: my father lifting me up in his arms, then casting me—long and lean as a baited line—into those harrowing waves. And when I came up for air, breaking (as they say) *the surface*, I smiled—despite the piercing cold, despite the unstoppable force and its untraceable source—and begged him to throw me back again like a bad catch, like a fish not worthy of nets. "Every summer we came here as kids, sometimes in the winters, too. And regardless of season, my dad would rise every morning, run down from the house or hotel, and dive headfirst into this surf."

I watch a cloud pass over my father's eyes, his reminiscence gentle at first, then the sudden turn of the tide. "He would have loved you so much. I'll never understand why God took him from us."

So grief is also a wave. I knew this then, even before I knew it.

The ocean becomes my first rubric for analysis. While I learn not to take the sea for granted, I grow instead to interpret waves as axiomatic. Some study tea leaves or Tarot cards; others toy with sinister and supernatural crystals. I hypothesize sandcastles' temporality (metaphor for our mortality?) and the fate of message-laden bottles washed ashore. I am intrigued also by the conch shell, which traps the voice of the ocean inside. Alone in her kitchen, I raise my mother's Mexican import to my scrupulous ear and consider this phantom presence: the sea singing back to me in urgent proximity—its plea to be heard, its wish to be cherished.

In school, we are taught how water comprises a preponderance of the human body. "Seventy-eight percent in infants," my teacher recites, "though slightly less as we grow older."

And I think *yes, this makes sense also*, that we are like conch shells, replete with a rapturous ocean, pure liquefaction barely contained by such thin walls of skin. It's a wonder we hold anything in, our wrists taut with string, the bright balloon-moon always tugging. Children, as it should be, are closer to the sea: the younger we are, the more malleable our constitutions—the more amphibious our minds—capable of dwelling on land and in water at the same time; of being the water and the bridge that passes over: *a diffuse membrane*, like we learned in class. When I sit in the bath, scrubbing away sand and sediment, noticing the bronzed creases of an unintended tan, I discover a place in my body that draws the water in: portal of osmosis, of passage. Maybe I am a harbor, maybe a well, but I sense some obligation attached to anatomy—the way a ship, I imagine, in the aftermath of sinking, turns newly sentinel toward its fabled treasure.

Flash-forward: In first-year philosophy, I study Anaximander and his theories. I think, *yes, this makes sense also*. Of course the cosmos evolved out of chaos. Of course there was this "primordial mass," this *apeiron*—like the given in math, from which we proceed to solve problems, give proof. How natural it seemed that our origins should be traced to the sea, to some mythic form between fish and human being. *Mermaid*, I will sketch in my notebook, with a satisfied sigh. I will think how I knew this, even before I knew it.

Flashback: At age eleven, I suffer another aquatic epiphany. This time, less existential: diagnosis of irreparable damage. My parents do not truly love each other—my father, a shell who has long since lost his music; my mother, a brazen moon. I watch while they pantomime perfection for the neighbors, then fold again into their separate, scalloped spheres. Is this because she does not love the ocean enough? Because he cleaves to its currents with his fierce and futile faith?

Or perhaps this trouble resides with origins. When my mother was small, she dove into a shallow pool, striking her head on concrete. As she describes it, the world grew dim; she felt her future unhinge, her life slip slowly away. But a lifeguard went in after and rescued her; he stretched her out on the warm bricks and breathed heat back into her lungs. To this day, my mother never puts her head under water. She washes her hair in the sink and only takes baths, not showers.

It is this woman who secretly, then not-so-secretly, begrudges me my love of the sea. She desired a daughter more sessile than motile: the kind to wear a swimming cap, to cultivate a cool and smug coiffeur. "You come back looking like a limp mop, head full of chlorine or salt. How do you expect to find a husband like that? What man would ever look twice?" I know how I disappoint her, refusing to shop or stop to "touch up," longing still for the sting of those waves.

And as she begrudged me, she begrudged my father also. "Why Seaside? Why every summer? No, I don't love the breakers crashing over the rocks. No, I don't sleep better down there."

My parents do not believe in continental drift. They never pursue a divorce. In school I learn the word for supercontinent—as we were before (*apeiron*); as we can never hope to ever be again (*Pangaea*). Was there truly a time when the world was pure, some order to its great primordial mass? What seems more plausible is this splitting: of hairs first, then bones, and later, minds. We find ourselves divided, but there's a harsher word, which I struggle to wrap my lips around—*severed*. Will this be my future, straining to fill the vast quayside where the vestige of family should reside?

Even grief is a wave. Even the land floats away as sandpipers peck at the crabs.

. . .

*Anaximander believed that there arose from heated water and earth either fish or animals very like fish. In these humans grew and were kept inside as embryos until puberty. Finally, they burst, and men and women came forth already able to nourish themselves.*

My preferred creation myth, my pre-Socratic love affair—this first man to present a reasonable map of the world. It was mostly ocean, yes? The way *we* are mostly ocean, our cells shed and cast off from us like land? In the end, perhaps it is not dust we are returned to after all. What if we had hatched from the bodies of our predecessors? What if all this talk of warm blood and mammalian life-course was nothing but a light show, spectral and short-lived?

As a child, how I longed for Jonah's whale. *Come, big fish,* I'd invoke him, almost as a prayer. *Come here and swallow me whole. Don't spit me back again until I'm ready to walk in this world.* But how would I walk without stumbling? So much of the time I gathered my breath in my chest, holding it there in anticipation—what fresh terror? what frantic joy? And always I feared the X-ray's threat, where instead of a thick fist thumping my ribs, the doctors would discover my heart was tragically webbed.

In the belly of Jonah's whale, or pleasantly adrift on Noah's catamaran (not a dove or an olive branch in sight), or there in my dream house perched high on barnacled pilings overlooking Alki Beach—in such places, I would know at last that sanctuary I could only simulate in my small porcelain tub, with my long legs spilling over, my head intermittently submerged. Then, my mother would come in, roll up her sleeves, delve her hands deep under the suds, and scrub my skull fiercely, determined to turn me clean. Once, detained at a meeting, she asked my father to act in her stead. He tapped at the door, tentative. I was maybe nine or ten. I should have been washing my own head. Still, my mother insisted. She didn't like me unsupervised in the tub. I think she pictured me there like Ophelia, feared me breathless and silent as the Lady of Shalott.

Peeking his head in, a turtle appraising from the safety of his shell, my father instructed: "Cover up."

I looked around. "Cover what?"

Adamant: "Just cover up."

The suds were melting, but the water was murky: my dead cells sloughed off in a mixture of soap and indifference. "I don't know—"

"Here—" He tossed me a small square of terry cloth from the closet in the hall. "Put it over your—the place between your legs."

Young Eve in retrograde, my small face falling. I sat still with my thighs pressed tight together, the cloth pulled taut across my—

But where the word should have been, there was only a sinkhole, like those we found on geoduck hunts where the reticent clams were hiding. In time, I would come to postulate a meaning to this place—*delta, estuary*—as in "alluvial region at the mouth of a river, usually triangular in shape"; as in "the wide lower course of a river where its currents are met by the tides."

Maybe this moment draws a line in the sand: *before*, when I was only a girl, prepubescent; *after*, when the mermaid fantasy unfolds. On the cusp of an essential knowingness, consumed by longing and loneliness, I understood myself then as the bearer of a body, the way a supplicant bears a cup. Something about shame, something about chalice: all that I was and all that I might contain. I could not conceive of existing without it (where that fluid and fleeting soul?), yet I could not reconcile possessing it, or being as it were, possessed *by* it. What to make of my body and our uneasy Cartesian split? Houses had shutters, and castles had moats, but where were my bunkers, where my crenellations? How to be hidden and what to preserve? Slowly, the sailor's jaunty slipknot, fastening surrender to survival.

Flash-forward: In high school, our spring fling takes place at the Seattle Aquarium. Having failed to muster strong feelings for any particular boy, my companion is preselected: son of a family friend, skinny and silent and paralyzed by fear of the female form. He can hardly bear to touch me, and his hands shake as they come to rest on my waist, as we oscillate in time to the music. I can hardly blame him for his trepidation, for I too am terrified by the thought of my body. *Vase-me*: breakable, vulnerable. *Canteen-me*: thirst-quenching; capable of being filled up.

In the blue room of the aquarium, where bodies turned silhouette and inhibitions slackened, we spun on an axis of glass. Windows for ceiling and windows for walls; behind them, the salt-gilt flux of the sea. I let my head fall to the crest of his shoulder, as the fins encircled us and the shadows fell; as the strangers groped and glided through dusky light and a lingering musk of cologne. I could see then (in the hypothetical heat) *wanting* to be coupled, as in the two-become-one; as in the jigsaw nature of the gendered puzzle: recondite aperture, aching to be plugged.

Flashback: "When I grow up, I want to be a mermaid." The other children laugh. "I'm serious," I say, lips fixed and fingers folded. Our field trip to the Waterfront includes visits to the Seattle Aquarium and a tour of a ship in port.

I have my galoshes and my purple polka-dot umbrella. I have also my notebook in a Ziploc bag, for field trips require field notes.

Wandering from room to room, I search for a creature with a human face but fins in place of her legs. Without these, I reason, there is no possibility of puncture: no crossing them the way good girls ought and tugging my short skirts down. My mother says, "Many a good girl has gone bad over spreading her legs too soon." And while I can't quite grasp her meaning, can't quite quantify these nebula—*gone bad, too soon*—a new sentiment hangs in the air between us, *such that* (a delta in math) whatever transgression, whatever temptation, I will have no one and only myself to blame.

Instead of mermaids, I find the octopus—recalcitrant, reserved—curled against a quiet corner of the glass. He is small and solitary, his tentacles a monstrous wad of burnt-orange and mayonnaise-white. I am mesmerized. In my notebook, I copy: *Hectocotylus, one of eight tentacles, functions as a kind of "third arm." Some open-ocean octopi have a unique form of reproduction. The tiny male's modified arm breaks off during mating and remains inside the mantle cavity of its mate. In this way, scientists have quipped that it is the male octopus, not the female, that loses its virginity.*

Flash-forward: To my friend, before roll call. "I know this is a strange question, but have you ever wondered how mermaids make love?"

"No. But I have wondered how they have sex."

Then also, I was mesmerized. It had not occurred to me prior to that moment that these phrases might refer to different things.

. . .

Flashback: We are on the ship now, having boarded the sturdy starboard ladder and squeezed tightly together—children, teachers, and chaperones— inside the musty hold. "Where is the plank?" I demand, thinking of Tiger Lily, her long braid and proud head, unbowed. But it's not a pirate ship, so there's no black flag waving its crossbones and skull, no plank for prisoners to walk or crow's nest for scouting the sea. Feeling cheated, I follow the rest of the girls into a renovated women's room, its sign a triangular woman in an unmistakable dress, her two legs superimposed into one.

"Do you have to go?" Mrs. Blaschke asks, and I shake my head no. "OK then. Wait right here."

As she steps into the stall, hanging her parka on the silver hook, spinning the thick roll of paper, I wander to the vending machine there on the wall and reach for a box of candy. Only it isn't candy, and I show it to Janna, who is washing her hands; to Erica, who is lacing up her shoes.

"What is that?"

"Some kind of bandage," I say. "It's so big it's probably in case you get a concussion."

I stretch the thick Kotex strip my full forehead's length, utter a cotton-soft sigh of relief. Soon, the other girls follow suit, and we are all caressing our cheeks and wrapping our hands with these slender islands of Kotex. When she emerges from her bathroom stall, Mrs. Blaschke gapes at the mouth, but instead of a scream, she snatches our bounty away.

"What is it with you?" her fine-toothed disdain, staring me square in the eye. "Why is enough never enough? Why must you always make waves?"

"I thought it was candy," I plead.

"We'll have you sit back on the bus till we're done."

"But I really thought it was candy. . . ."

At home in the house without shutters, in the castle without a moat, I sit on my mother's bed, patiently rocking.

"Something happened today," I say. And suddenly, I am filled to brimming then spilling, the harsh capsize of my incontestably curious body. "There were boxes in the bathroom on the boat, and I opened one while Mrs. Blaschke was in the stall. And it wasn't candy like I thought but a big soft raft of some kind. I thought it was a bandage. I thought—but then Mrs. Blaschke came back and got really angry with me."

"It wasn't your fault."

Taken aback by her tenderness: "But I opened the box."

"You didn't know what it was."

"No—but I wanted to." Cautiously: "I *still* want to."

"Mrs. Blaschke didn't explain it to you?"

I shake my head no. "Can you?"


My mother, who is also a teacher and a thespian, speaks deliberately, dramatically. When I am twelve or thirteen, she says, sometime in my early adolescence, I will discover the wound in my body. It's nothing I can prevent or should fear; women are simply born wounded. And I think, *yes, this makes sense also*, that we are like conch shells; of course, *postlapsarian*, the cosmos orchestrates this pained and gendered order.

And every month the healing wound is ripped open again, spilling its red sea of anguish. The Bible foretold as much: Eve's suffering in childbirth "greatly increased," her descendants punished *by* the body *for* the body—God's false pantomime of justice.

"When you are bleeding," my mother explains, "you need something to absorb the menses. Some women use tampons, which go inside, but others use sanitary napkins, which can be belted to the outside of your body. What you found in the bathroom today was a sanitary napkin, and when the time comes, that is what you will wear."

"How long will it last?" I ask, lips quivering now.

"Several days out of every month. The exact duration differs for everyone. But during this time, you should stay indoors and not overexert yourself. Many women have swelling and soreness and a terrible throbbing in the abdomen called menstrual cramps. Oh, and—" she says it offhandedly, as though it won't matter at all, "you can't swim during menstruation."

"But, Mom! I can't go several days out of every month without swimming!" I imagine our summers at Seaside, my father riding the waves without me, and the tears well up in my eyes.

"It's not the end of the world," she replies. "Some women who wear tampons go swimming during their cycles, but it's highly unsafe and unadvisable.

Tampons are dangerous and improper, particularly for virgins, and I won't permit it." She sighs and pats my knee. "And without a tampon, well—you can't have blood in the water."

So grief is a wave also. I knew this then, even before I knew it.

Afterward, I lay on my little raft of a bed, the collapsed sail of my body crippled with sorrow and sobbing. "I should have been a boy! I should have been a boy!" Thinking of Robin Hood and Peter Pan, the Woodsman with hatchet in hand, even the bland Prince Charming. But while I envied them the sealed compartments of their bodies, their bloodless moons and stalwart seasons, I was not so willing to relinquish my femaleness all together. Women, I reasoned, were much more interesting, or so I had always perceived them. The pure functionality of the male form, the virility that seemed to substitute for cunning or even courage in many stories I read, did not provide a compelling endorsement. So the mantra switches again from men to mermaids: what I should have been, what I wished I could still become. How else to retain the innate power and privilege of womanhood without surrendering a single moment of my life in the sea?

I tell my father I want to scuba dive. Snorkeling, he says, would be a better way to start. "But I want the wet suit," I explain, drawn to its pleasing androgyny, "and the oxygen tank. I want to go deep and not have to resurface for hours."

Instead, when my birthday comes, I receive flippers, a mask, and a snorkel. "You can go about three feet under with that one," he beams. "You can practice in the swimming pool and work up to a larger body of water."

I try, but I always descend too far, choking as water floods my mouth and hating how everyone can see me skimming the surface. I crave incognito, the full katabasis of a genuine sea creature.

"When do you think I might be ready for deep-sea diving?"

My father is a kind man, patient but overprotective. He explains that diving is dangerous; he can't reconcile himself to letting me go too deep. "But why not? What are you afraid is going to happen?"

"It isn't the way you might think," he says. "If you were down there and couldn't breathe—if something went wrong with your tank—you couldn't swim quickly to the surface. Depending how far down you are, your ascent has to be calculated, slow. Otherwise, you'll get the bends, and your lungs will explode."

"The bends?" I repeat.

"Yes; it's something that happens when divers rise to the surface too quickly. It's best to avoid depth of that kind all together."

Flash-forward: I ask the boy I am seeing—the one I want desperately to love—if he will write a poem for me. "Aren't those supposed to be unsolicited?" he quips, and I blush, but he writes it anyway. Ben is shy also; we sleep together, close but unconsummated. He chooses a blue page in my small book, arranges his words carefully, and leaves before I can read what he has written.

And though he doesn't know about my years of longing for aquatic exile, the Tampax I hoard under my bed but can't quite bring myself to unwrap, or the way I sometimes (still) play Virginia Woolf in my bathtub, holding my breath as long as I can, invoking either death or transformation, he knows enough to hypothesize a love of full immersion:

*Blue love, like the deep cerulean seas;*
*Fathoms immeasurable, sinking forever through the waters of your soul.*
*And I know that if I try to surface, I will only get the bends.*

*So I don't.*

*Seeking instead the bed of a bottomless ocean.*
*Seeking infinity in your embrace.*

As I wash up on the soft shore of the morning—body intact, heart irreversibly fractured—I feel my legs, strong and sturdy, and the longing for fins recedes a little further. I am (for that moment) gill-less, guilt-less, without guile or regret.

Like the given in math, from which we proceed to solve problems, give proof.

# A Life on Land

In every life, there comes a moment of emergence: the skin shed, the scales fallen. To be born is to plummet headlong into an unfamiliar sea. No parachutes. No patiently attending skiffs. But let it be said, and forthright: there is no disappointment in the water. It's trying to get back, all the fraught momentum hurling you forward, the twist of the will to resist. Not the undertow, no—something stronger: call it *the overhaul*; call it *the revision*. To survive is to wash up on this shore.

Remember the weightlessness of bodies in the childhood pool—how we carried each other, dizzy hours on end? No one was burdened then by the physicality of form, the learned helplessness of floating in jellyfish pose or sculling on our backs beneath a tentative sun. I understand now the hard-syllabled heft of this word: *land*. My cleft tongue can barely lift it. Is land moving? If so, we have *islands*. Pangaea cracked; solidarities fractured. We can stand on the land and feel our feet affix as they never did in liquid. As they never could. A morose, solid feeling creeps in: boulders and fossils, the petrified longings in each of us. Set into cliffsides; carved into stones. It's enough to make anyone look back: pillars of salt, pillars of sand, get me to the glass-gilt sea!

When we left the West Coast, it was without spectacle—so unlike us—unsentimental, abrupt. We smoked the last of our weed and slept on the spartan floor. I may have crawled into your sleeping bag, sometime around sunrise. On waking, we loaded the last of our lives into the car. No one was watching, but we felt furtive, suddenly shy. "Try not to look at the world like you're making a memory of it," we said, all the while scouring that panorama for a blessing, gazing after the last seagull like a portrait of our vanishing past. I wondered then if I would ever write about it. I wondered—sailing down Interstate 5, then 101 for a spell, then back again to a skein of concrete cities we had never seen, and veering off into the desert for good.

This now did not exist then. The law of the land is learning how to build things. The law of the land is shelter wrought from ruins.

Five years ago, in spring. Out till all hours. Chocolate, caffeine, and nicotine. Blue veins taut to bursting beneath the startled skin. It was like this. I said, "Look, I love you." I said, "Look at the moon, and look at me. Tell me one of us is lying."

Lake Samish and the shower and the bath and the bed—I get ahead of myself. First, there were tears. First, there was your tiny garden and the hummingbirds coalescing under the stairs. And the evening chill that requires just the lightest of jackets. And the back row of the cinema, where we were all hands and mouths without words.

I had loved men before. Or. I had been loved by men before. Or. I had been confused before, about the heart and its improbable machinations, its imponderable flux. Back in Catholic school, we read *The Canterbury Tales*. I thought I was in love with Chaucer. And there was a brooch the nun wore in the story Chaucer told through and about her. The brooch was engraved *Amor Vincit Omnia*, and Sister Mary Annette explained: "Latin, for *Love Conquers All*."

Afterward, I had a moment outside myself and time, a moment untouched by custom and the future's heavy hand. In this moment, I thought: "Someday, when I propose, I'll give my lover a ring with these words chiseled inside." It gave me chills to imagine: those silver bands, that secret language, our life together liquid as mercury in a vial.

It's trying to get back to that moment, before the glass breaks and the little gendered beads scatter across the floor. Trying to get back to a pure thought, to a dream of love beyond chromosomes and social configurations. I did not want to be a man. I did not want to be with a man. My verbs were wrong and also my prepositions. Under water, we had no use for pockets. On land, I learned it was possible to tuck desire away.

"You had to know this would change things," my best friend said. She was married and living in California under a wild orange tree that lavished her lawn with fruit.

"Love is love," I murmured. "I love her; she loves me. What more do you want from me?"

"I just never—I never pictured you with a woman. I just never saw you that way."

"What way?"

Exasperated, she spat out the word: "As gay!"

"I didn't say I was gay, and I *never* said I was straight."

"That's absurd. You dated men! You were engaged to be married! If that isn't straight, then I don't know what is."

I didn't know either. And the silence between us swelled until we became, as she forecasted, *apples and oranges*. Her world with its arrows; mine with its harps and bows.

*Never*, a new wave cresting our story, the pages soaked and pecked apart by birds. The law of the land is quake and rupture. The law of the land is a litany of oranges, falling.

We had entered the nowhere world: no gas stations, no cell phone service, no certain end to the sprawling, sun-laden days. Forget about the birds we knew, forget about the trees. Someone's pink sofa just shy of the roadside; a few miles past, the matching ottoman; and off in the distance, a recliner capsized between cacti. We laugh, but it becomes a metaphor for the way we lose things slowly, these incremental progressions of grief despite the spectral backdrop of joy.

. . .

In Nevada, it seemed possible we might drown on land—*on* it and *in* it—swallowed up as we were in the brown dust, and still the bright road's gleaming extravagance. Nothing muted, nothing tamed. We watched a storm gather on this horizon. She had seen tornadoes, growing up; I had seen *The Wizard of Oz.* A sound, like sheet metal shaken in a school play—to give the effect of rain, to make the audience believe it. Then, the puckered sky split, and we drove into the downturned mouth of an ocean, gushing over us like a fickle friend. No choice but to keep going: her hand in my hand, a cigarette's glow; the landscape a flood of torn pockets.

June 26, 2003. Breakfast in Reno. Our first glimpse of the morning news. One caption read—"American Flags Adorn Canal Street!" Another—"Lawrence v. Texas Overturned!" I salted my eggs; I buttered my bread; I read the paper in silence. Afterward:

"So this means?"

"People are entitled to sexual privacy. So long as it's consensual, they can do as they please."

"And we—"

"—are also free to do as we please." You smiled at me over the white rim of your coffee.

"Now, but not then. Not yesterday? Or last year?" The lake, the shower, the bath, the bed. . . . "Were we *criminals*, all this time, without knowing?"

"The laws were on the books. In most cases, they weren't even enforced. And now they can't be. End of story."

Which is also, of course, the beginning of one: a sudden, irrefutable implication. I went to the washroom; I scrubbed newsprint from my hands; I saw myself transfigured in the mirror. One of the Others now—not the storyteller or the commentator, but she about whom the comments are made.

No one aspires to this: your life contested, your love condemned, a court convened to discuss your rights and merits. The law of the land isn't written in these books. The law of the land is a choke hold and a phonograph: makes you listen to everything you miss.

I remember the first morning after. We composed a grocery list. You got dressed and went reluctantly to class. I closed my eyes and let your scent surround.

Later, the world seemed fresh and holy as I stepped outside—still the world I knew, but softer in my altered light. There I was, in the supermarket, strolling through the aisles, feeling myself newly inhabit my form. Not a hostile place, this world. The comforting smiles of strangers. Their raw approval of my small and gentle life, my tall baguette and ripening green bananas. "Did you find everything you were looking for today?" And I did, and I had, and I thanked him—not knowing this moment too was a vial, not picturing this future, broken and given for us.

Let me dip the ladle further down in time. Let me tell you about the family I was destined to leave behind. There's a word for this too—*estrangement*. A word that, not unlike erosion, happens over time, gradual and irreparable as any sedimentary story. Here, I'll show you. Imagine you are walking on the shore, barefoot, with the cuffs of your trousers rolled up, a soft sea breeze in your hair. You notice a trail of pebbles, a jumble of agates and crushed shells. You are curious about the workings of this ocean: how it breaks whole colonies apart; how it pantomimes this daily regimen of displacement, synchronized by the shifting of the tides. Soon, you are collecting its castoffs. One by one, small stones and blunted glass accumulate in your pockets. You are not thinking then about culminations. You are not thinking then about endings. You want only for simple, reasonable things: a shower and a cup of chowder, a hot water bottle tucked at the base of your bed.

Is this too much to ask? Are you being punished for impudence? An unwitting thief, your pockets tear open. In some versions, your pockets fall off and are carried away by cormorants, terns. The lost contents of the pockets, irredeemable now. The windbreaker or blazer, split open at its seams. Even the roses on the dunes billow differently, and you will not look back when the sun drops behind the mountains. Sunsets are spoiled forever.

I didn't know how far apace we were, how dangerous my silence must have seemed. I was reveling when the telephone rang. I was learning myself new in the mirror of my lover's body, beneath the veil of her extravagant hair.

"Your father's on the phone for you."
"My father?"
"That's what he said."
Our eyes bright and moist as morning dew.

"Hello? Dad? Has something happened?"
"Where are you?"
"Where are *you*?"
"Julie, your mother and I have been worried sick. We know you've been avoiding us. We came all this way to talk with you, only to find you aren't where you're supposed to be."
"It's Saturday morning. I'm twenty-two years old. Where exactly am I *supposed* to be?"
"Your mother's made sandwiches. We've done what we could to straighten up your place. Is it possible you don't even own a broom?"
Sitting up now, my pert toes on the cold floor, gooseflesh and trembling. "Are you saying you're *in* my apartment? How in the world did you get in?"
"That's really beside the point, isn't it? The real question is—will your friend bring you home, or do I have to come over there and get you?"

The law of the land is a trial of errors. The law of the land is a gavel in your father's hand.

We learned about intentions early on: how the will must be muscle, not bone. Nebraska was a long, smooth space on our map. We meant to drive through and move on. Picture us: two women in a station wagon with out-of-state plates, housewares and camping gear strapped to the roof of our car. Anything but inconspicuous. Anyones but the ones who belonged.

. . .

We were not prepared for the prairie. We were not prepared for the bristling heat and the buckling bridge and no room for us at the inns. Sturgis season, and the orange DETOUR signs, ominous on the outskirts of Sidney. I said, "Maybe we ought to look at that map again." You said, "Maybe we ought to turn around." So when we saw the junction at 76, we didn't ask questions. I lit a cigarette, and you steered the car: our slow, urgent descent into Colorado.

The absence of water began as a fact. We ventured inland, and the land overcame us. We attended to the briny, furrowed curvatures of unfamiliar earth, the tireless highways, the dervishes of dust and dirt. Like all tourists, we took a certain pleasure in this foreignness. We aspired to taste, savor, and consume it. We kept photographic evidence to sustain us, long after the flavor was gone.

But in time, we discovered we were not tourists at all. We did not share their luxury of leave-taking and home-coming: those Libra scales balanced by return. In departing, we had surrendered our part in one particular history, collapsing our tent, kicking sand on our flickering fire.

Now the absence of water becomes mythical, like the myth of progress, like the myth of pulled stakes and kempt pathways. This is what being landlocked looks like: a license plate instead of a mailing address; a station wagon instead of a residence; a recalcitrant cell phone instead of a land line, so most of the time you can't be reached; most of the time a vague message reports "out of area," or more to the point, "no service."

That night: our katabasis from 80 to 76, disjuncture of our chosen path. We cracked the windows to let out the smoke, to snuff out the fire, and that's when we heard it—the prairie's howl, the disembodied voice of the wind. And I don't mind telling you I was scared then. Every hair on my neck stood stiff, and my knuckles went pale. I thought of Brandon Teena; I thought of Matthew Shepard: more landlocked bodies in a waterless world. I thought of every time we asked for separate beds, and every time we smiled and passed for sisters. I thought too of the husband I nearly once had: his large body, his masterful hands. Was it any wonder that I had confused them: the twinned compass, safety and love?

Had it been him, had we roved together across this severe and mysterious country, I would have thought nothing of where we slept, where we drove. I would have been a woman attached to a man, our lives interlocking, our cruise controlled. I would have tipped back my seat and fallen into storybook sleep, waking to a kiss in Denver at dawn.

The law of the land is that nothing is promised: not where you are going, not where you have been. The law of the land is a still point. The truth is how you appear.

Remember the slow, smooth, unimpeaching hypothesis of water? Remember when anything was possible, simply because it had been conjured by the mind? In college, I learned the seductive power of this subjunctive, floating through my days on a docile little raft of *what if?* I had made no commitments to my own body, no promises to the bodies of others. We remained hypothetical also—they and I—treading through the anteroom of pleasure, testing the port and starboard of a first and furtive touch.

What I loved then was ballroom dancing, with its scripted flourishes and safely routinized turns. I had no significant romantic prospects, and my parents and I were not yet formally estranged. This was my before-life, my hunkering down in the snowy-deep antecedent of now. So much abuzz beneath my studious skin; so much held diligently at bay. And my parents, who did not know me but wanted to love me—fearfully and without knowing how—took me with them on hiatus in Harrison Hot Springs, a secluded resort town set against the snowbrushed mountains of British Columbia.

Here I was to practice my heterosexuality, to be inducted into a world of affluent married couples who read by the fire, took tea at three, and wandered through sculpted gardens at sunset, arm in arm. Love, I learned, could be a performance, as complex and elegant as the waltzes I had studied or the tangos or the West Coast swing.

One night in the Copper Room, having dressed for dinner, having taken our places around a linen-covered table beneath the dim lights of the dance floor, we observed the young pairings of boy and girl, in processional, toward the outdoor canopy and profuse flower arrangements of Prom. I understood as all eyes shifted to the windows that being observed in courtship is as crucial as the courtship itself.

A young woman had come solo and stood fidgeting with her wrist cor-sage of roses: tiny and yellow, perhaps given to her by a loving mother or a pushing friend, someone who insisted she should "get out there," "make her presence known." Her shoulders were fair and fleshy, her arms admirably freckled, and her eyes downturned, trying to pretend she didn't notice being noticed alone.

I wanted to dance with her. I can tell you that now because we are strang-ers, and I have discovered that strangers, often, are safer than friends, kinder than even those we call "loved ones." They have less invested in us; therefore, they have far less to lose.

But my mother, seeing her tall and awkward in a yellow gown, perhaps remembering me only a year or two before—tall and awkward in a yellow gown, leaning on the arm of a short and brooding boy—could not resist the opportu-nity to comment.

"What a shame," she whispered, tearing open a soft white roll and coarsely swiping it with the cold and scalloped butter.

"I never understood that expression. Who is it who's supposed to be ashamed?"

"You and your words. Honestly. Sometimes I don't know how we put up with you."

I sipped my water. I held small shards of ice between my teeth.

"It's just a sadness, that's all. No mother wants that for her child."

Deliberately now: "To what does the *that* in your sentence refer?"

Her eyes clamped on my face, bitter and blue. "Wake up, darling. These are the years when matches are made, and nobody likes a portly princess."

We all go on, of course. Origins determine nothing but the nature of our nostalgia, the memorable excerpts of our most tragic dreams. The law of the land is crevice and crack. Step over the line, and the motherland will break back.

In Arkansas, it finally happened. I wonder sometimes if our fear made it so, if our fear in fact made it inevitable. Back in Bellingham, when we still had a bed to sleep in and closets to open and drawers to fill and four chairs arranged around a table in that grown-up, purposive way—even a small window from the corner of the shower where you could catch a glimpse of downtown lights and of the glistening Bellingham Bay—we read an article in one of the papers. Two women, known to be lovers, had been found murdered and heaped in the back of their flatbed truck, somewhere in rural Oregon.

This story had rattled us. Police refused to comment as to whether these women had been victims of a "hate crime." Vigils were held. Candles sunk to the ground in waxy puddles.

And here we were, miles from eastern Oregon and from any horizon that resembled our home. We stopped for water and chocolate bars at a gas station eighty miles west of Little Rock. We set arbitrary goals, deciding we would reach the capital before turning in for the night.

Our spirits were high, and the hot evening air poured pleasantly through the windows, and we sang along with the radio, oblivious at first to the white van that rode up close on our bumper, hovered awhile, then slipped back into the stream of cars. Then night fell, with a thud like fruit overburdening the tree, and we noticed a set of headlights closing in, the high beams flooding our space, straining our eyes.

. . .

I pressed my foot down harder on the gas; the white van accelerated in tandem. I braked softly, and the white van did not attempt to go around. Ahead, signs indicated the road would narrow: one lane between rows of cones.

"I'm not imagining this?" I asked, palms sticky on the wheel, body hunching forward to shield my eyes from the torrents of light.

"No. They're following us. I don't know why, but they won't let up. They just keep inching closer."

We drove miles like this, snaking between abutments and ditches, sometimes with barriers lining both sides of the road. Then, the highway would open for a little while, four lanes again with room for passing. We moved into the right; they followed, tight as if a tether bound us. Again into the left, at prodigious speeds; they were never more than a few feet behind.

"How would they know? How could they know?" I murmured, believing all intended crimes must be hate crimes, grieving our ghostly disappearance somewhere in rural Arkansas.

In the end, we saw a sign for the Highway Patrol. We followed the smooth black road off the interstate, drawing up to a bustling BP. The white van was behind us all the way, revving its engine, its lights growing brighter in our mirror. We sat paralyzed in the car outside the convenience store doorway, while the white van perched across the parking lot at a self-service pump. We couldn't make out the figures in front. No one ever stepped out to get gas.

The standoff that followed may have lasted several minutes. It may have also lasted close to an hour. We clutched the phone in our shared hands—as if it held power: a totem to protect us from harm. "If they get out," we agreed, "we'll run inside." Again and again: appraising the distance between ourselves and the door.

Eventually, the white van revved its engine. Defeated, it roared back out on the road. We couldn't see the license plate, nor did we care to. Hot tears burned under my eyelids. That night at a nicer hotel—with rooms you enter through the lobby, and a clerk on desk duty twenty-four hours—I slept deeper than ever, writhing through dreams of pursuit and disaster. You lay awake, stroking my hair, every other minute to the window.

The law of the land is a series of scenes: the obscene, the unseen, and the *mise-en-scène*. When it comes, dawn is a white flag waving. Call it *the overhaul*. Call it *the revision*.

A future, it comforts me to remember, is something we make up as we go along. And the forks in the road (and the knives and the spoons . . . ) present their own post hoc gratifications. The counterpoint to *what if?* is a bit more poignant. Instead of the speculative future, let's call it the preemptive past. The *might have been*. The *could have been*. The *wasn't*.

Plenty of people believed the hot springs possessed healing powers. On a trail walk with my parents, we saw warning signs about mountain lions, known to wander too close to the grounds. After dinner and dancing, I returned to our room to read. I had hidden John Updike's *Couples* in the satin upper fold of my suitcase. What a voyeur I was—into the secret lives of philandering New England heterosexuals!

But my parents went down to the lobby, well past their usual bedtime. They sat at a solitary table playing cards, only to burst back into the room an hour later.

"Back so soon?" I asked, slipping the tawdry hardback under my covers.

"You won't believe it!" my father cried. I could see, from across the room, his hands were shaking.

My mother paced back and forth, swabbing her makeup with a cotton ball. "I've never been so terrified in all my life. And to think we pay good money to stay here!"

"What happened?"

"Julie, I tell you, we were sitting not more than a few yards from the door, and suddenly your mother felt a chill. We looked back, and the sliding doors were open, and we couldn't figure out why, and then we realized that someone must have triggered them from outside."

"And?" I saw the sincerity in his face; I watched the panic wafting off of her in waves.

"Well, there were these eyes, flickering in the dark. We couldn't see what they were at first, but Julie—it was a mountain lion, standing right there in the doorway. We're lucky we got away."

That night, after they were asleep, I crept down to the lobby. I regarded the straight-backed chairs, coupled in front of the fireplaces; the empty carts for the next day's tea service; the cocktail lounge with its pyramid of translucent martini glasses.

I think I was there because I have a morbid imagination. I think I was there because I half wanted my own encounter with that brazen cat, so bold as to trespass in a land where citizens could buy themselves out of anything but death. I half wanted to commend him for striking fear in their hearts with only the faintest suggestion of harm. It meant they were alive, and perhaps I also needed to feel that surge in my blood, an affirmation I had something to live for.

I half wanted also to opt out of my life, so tame and unrequited; to die tragically, as all my literary heroines had done with such aplomb. But the truth, which is also a myth of its own protective making, goes a shade darker. If my parents had died—out of the blue, in a "freak incident" no one would have ever believed—I might have spared them a different, already foreshadowed pain: that spearhead of disappointment as I became everything they detested and nothing they had ever dreamed.

Maybe I was more powerful than even that mountain lion. Maybe I was more dangerous in the menacing of incidental prey. *What a shame*, all the couples would have murmured in the aftermath, and that word—*shame*—would have risen up in an omniscient-third sort of way, teaching me I could not be held accountable; urging me to heal myself, to learn how to walk away.

. . .

The law of the land is covert investigation, explicit introspection. The law of the land is a foray into how the land lies.

When we reached Ohio, we were tired of driving, tired of stopping, tired of our own scratchy voices and soft-pack cigarettes and filtered music. We had wanted to see more of the world, and in this pursuit, we succeeded. Cincinnati loomed old and grand over the same Ohio River we would follow all the way to Pittsburgh. *How different could they be?* we wondered—both industrial towns in a post-industry age, engaged in their own projects of overhaul, revision.

But our destination was that delta, five hours northeast, unknown to both of us except from the backs of ketchup bottles we used to peruse in the Little Cheerful Café. I had grown up so accustomed to beauty that Ohio seemed a little much to bear, as if the last nail in a coffin of solid things, in the consecration of my life and death as a fugitive. We were about to pitch tents; we were about to build fires. The long days of traveling would be over, and we could aspire then to be tourists again—with someplace to leave, someplace to return to.

"You know what I was just thinking?" You shook your head, eyes steady on the weed-frilled road. "I was thinking how it doesn't make sense to me that when people put messages in bottles they actually trusted their messages would arrive."

"Maybe it had nothing to do with trust. If you're stranded at sea, it might be the only prospect you have of reaching land—even figuratively."

"I know, but those are the same circumstances in which people who don't usually pray utter prayers. . . . Maybe it's not about whether the message ever gets anywhere—because if you're going to sink, you're going to sink—but at least you had a chance to put into words what you were thinking."

"Postal system too reliable for you?"

"In a way, yes. Because I'm not sure I want my parents to know where we are. But there are things I would say to them, if I were adrift with a cork, a bottle, and some waves."

. . .

July 4, 2003. A hypothetical letter. *Dear Mom and Dad. Since there's not much chance this letter will ever reach you, I can speak freely at last—perhaps for the first time. Do you want to know the strange thing about estrangement? Sometimes it feels like we were so much farther apart, living in the same house, breaking bread at a common table, combing the same beaches on Saturday afternoons, than it does right now, all these miles away, and more than miles. I wonder sometimes if I can only really love you at a distance, where the discrepancy between everything I miss (as in the pure nostalgia) and everything I've missed (as in the great absences of my life) can coalesce, finally—into one peaceful wish that we each have done the best we know how and that all of us will continue a long, patient walk onto the promontory of the future.*

In Denver, after driving all night and coming into the sunrise at just the right moment, we found a diner that, in the right light, resembled our old Little Cheerful. We ate crisp bacon and sourdough toast and Denver omelets, which made us chuckle in spite of ourselves. I can't call it a premonition, but a sense of peace settled over me in that restaurant. Despite everything that followed, I was also puffed up a little inside, as if I had feathers and a long grand tail and a reason to hold on to my pride.

In the bathroom, on the last squeaky stall door, I wrote our names and made a heart and added the word "forever." I had never gotten to do that before, when everyone was signing yearbooks and carving the trunks of trees. And anything I had ever written in the soft pliable sand was so easily and predictably washed away.

The law of the land is marking your trails. You don't know when you will return, or if. Before long, you wish your memory were eidetic. Before too long, you wish for amnesia's tender salve. The law of the land is a set of spectacles and a Smith Corona: makes you study everything you miss.

We arrived in Pittsburgh during a thunderstorm. No evidence of a city, then passing through a tunnel, and suddenly she appeared. I like the custom of calling boats and places after women. Pittsburgh, like a debutante past her prime, reclined into the hills around her, wrinkled and wan with a poignant, ne'er-do-well gleam in her eyes. Water all around us, but also more bridges than I had ever seen, ferrying the traffic above and away from those shores.

"So—who did you dance with at Harrison Hot Springs? I've always wanted to know."

"With my father. Not many singles there and no one remotely close to my age."

"But you had a good time dancing?"

Thinking of the long dresses and the tall strappy shoes and feeling beautiful and appropriate in the gendered illusion of lead and follow: "I think I wanted the affirmation. I'm not terribly pleased with myself that it meant so much, but it did. After we danced, people would often stop by the table and remark what a lovely family we were or how most young people today didn't know the first thing about ballroom dancing. One of the members of the band—he must have been at least forty years old—would look at me when I was dancing, and I'd catch his eye over my father's shoulder, and I had this uncanny feeling that he wanted me. I didn't know what it was like to be wanted, and it had nothing to do with wanting him back, but his long glances and nods made me feel strangely powerful. Surely he wouldn't have reacted that way to anyone but a good heterosexual girl."

We were driving through the city that would become something akin to home, the place where we would hang our hats and stomp our boots in winter, the place where we would be broken again by insult and ignorance but also affirmed, in small ways, by a few kind and exceptional friends. Once, I caught myself humming a song from the old Harrison dance floor. I knew best the Frank Sinatra recording of it, which my father had kept and cherished: "I'm gonna sit right down and write myself a letter and make believe it came from you."

I had gone down to check the mail in our first Pittsburgh apartment: the row of metal boxes, the shiny silver key, my first authentic experience of privacy. Those words suddenly came back to me and I heard myself sing them in the hallway, trudging up the lonely stairs: "I'm gonna smile and say/I hope you're feeling better/I'll close with love the way you do/I'm gonna sit right down and write myself a letter/And make believe it came from you."

If you had known my address, if you had been able and willing to reach me, what would you have said? Perhaps something about hell, something about obligation, almost certainly something about betrayal. But in the song, the singer writes his own story. He has the privilege, this once, of telling himself exactly what he would most like to hear.

And from my parents, who did not read poems, who did not meditate on the intricacies of language, who were in fact brittle people afraid at every tremor of being broken, the finest letter I could imagine would be one acknowledging my life was not their jurisdiction, one acknowledging no way or reason to protect me from the person I had and needed to become.

I closed my eyes, leaning against our door, letting the sun flood my face through the skylight. The envelope would be simple and small with a Seattle postmark, perhaps the ink bubbled with rain for effect. And the slip of paper inside, recycled and lined, would be borrowed words from a poem I kept and cherished: *The longing is to be pure; what you get is to be changed.*

It occurs to me now that baptism has always been a significant ritual because no one feels pure enough on land. Here, in the last vestiges of industry, a city on the cusp of crisis (fiscal, ideological), I'm told stories of businessmen changing their shirts two and three times a day: the crisp white Oxfords, continually darkened with soot. Maybe we don't get to be cleansed. Maybe that is the ultimate lesson of land—understanding at last that you are smudged, that you have left your fingerprints everywhere, that you track mud through the house and through the rooms of your life, and dust accumulates on every smooth and furrowed surface.

"Look, I love you." A pocket sealed. The law of the land is learning to live as you are.

IV

# Black Fleece

*Does the grain of sand know it is a grain of sand?*
*Will secrets fly out of me when I break open?*
*Are the stars standing in any order?*
*Is supplication useful?*
—Mary Oliver

I am white today, white and khaki. I choose khaki because it is not a color any-one can contest or challenge. I am eighteen, clean and pressed: a neutral glide of cotton and canvas, tanned lines of open-toed shoes. It is one of those days I can feel my skin, the steam of self-awareness rising. My books I keep close to my chest, and with each cautious step, I force myself not to look down.

*It begins with a bee sting.*

I step, and the yellow jacket, winging his way toward clover, stymies, there in the soft sandal edge. I press down, he pokes up—we surprise each other. I hobble away; he crawls off to the grass and dies. A first time for both of us. My mother told me once she is allergic. She said my father is allergic, too. I am limping now, the sting having hardened into something like a pebble in my shoe, under my skin: rolling and shifting. I see a boy I know from class and ask him where the Health Center is. I don't remember his name; he reminds me. *Ben.* "I'll take you," he says, and offers to carry my bag. We walk together in si-lence toward a dark building shaded by maples; the sign reads "Health Center," and I go in, forgetting to thank him, feeling the pain move, the small vial of poison climbing the back of my legs. I am eighteen, remember. It is only by worry I live.

"May I help you?"

The woman at the desk is calm: sterile smile and talcum skin. I tell her my trouble.

"And you've never been stung before?" she inquires.

I tell her no, that if I had, this pain I'm sure I'd remember. She says, *Wait*. It is the longest word of my life, the one I wake to out of every dream. *I am tired of waiting.* She steps around the counter with latex gloves, a pillow, and a pack of ice.

"We'll prop your foot up," she directs. "Make sure the stinger is out. Now I don't want you to panic—there's probably nothing to worry about—but in some cases, if both parents are allergic . . . " inspecting me now for the stinger like a fragile thorn . . . "in some cases, there is anaphylactic shock."

The pain, rising like yeast to my brain. "What?"

She studies my wound, intently casual: "It's possible your heart may stop."

≈

Sister Rosemary, my favorite nun, writes in flourished cursive with a piece of grizzled chalk: *Christmas Party Tonight.*

I work for the school as a student ambassador, and each Christmas I don my black blouse, black skirt, black tights, black pointed-toe shoes, and that crimson cardigan with droopy buttons and silly badge. Patrons come to bid on Christmas trees and sip champagne until their pocketbooks turn loose as their mouths. The more outgoing girls have been assigned tea trays and serving spoons while the rest of us, like little mice who scamper unseen, sweep up crumbs in the kitchen or stand alone in the cloakroom, hanging and tagging each coat.

Ten-thirty, and I am tired already. Carolers croon in the hall. Sister Rosemary has come back to her classroom looking for masking tape to hold up the mistletoe. I smile at the irony, and she sees me—my shoulders slumped, my punch cup empty, my sweater set on the floor.

*I am tired of waiting.*

"I have something for you," she grins, approaches my station, closes the door. It is just us now, two celibates smiling: she who is nearly sixty, and I who have just turned fifteen.

"Every Christmas," says Sister, "I treat myself to one of these." And from her deep pocket she pulls out the strangest fruit I have ever seen: odd-bodied, a colorful, elegant rind. "Do you know what this is?"

I am thinking a gourd or a melon maybe, but I shake my head no.

*Pomegranate.* Suddenly, there is a knife in her hand, and she makes an incision so sharp and skillful I marvel she is a nun and not a surgeon. The juice squirts everywhere, reminiscent of communion wine or two summers' past, first blood. Her fingers are dripping with it, slick and red, and she is laughing and licking them, joyful as a schoolgirl with a popsicle.

She gives me some. "Don't worry if you spill, dear," Sister Rosemary gleams. "Black hides a multitude of sins." I put my mouth into the heart of the honeycomb, the dark beads full of sweetness, breaking open under the blade of my tongue.

"This is the only fruit," she says, "that cannot be eaten. You must simply devour it."

≈

*Have you ever thought how there is a kiss in everyone's mouth?*

≈

When my mother was sick, which was much of the time, my father discovered how easy it was to entertain me. "Give her something to hold," my mother had said. "If she has the world in her hands, she won't need to meddle with Other Things."

Sometimes the world was a quill pen, and I would practice, page after page, filling a guest book with my lonely name. Sometimes the world was a Magic Eight Ball, later denied because our church had decided *Magic was unchristian*. Before my father threw it out with the trash, I sat with that ball on my bed and kept asking, "Why can you only give me yes or no answers? Don't you know how boring that is?" *Yes. No. Maybe.*

I think of these three, *maybe* is the harshest word.

≈

They are roses soft as window curtains, pink in places but also yellow at the bud tips and the bowing stems. I remember what the woman told me in the flower shop—that if you touch them they wilt sooner, shriveling from fingers as they close up at night from the cold. I heard what she said. I was listening. But when her back was turned, I plunged my whole face into the blooms, fanning those petals over my cheeks like the gauzy soothe of cashmere. I touched them with my hungry hands.

≈

It was well after midnight when they brought me home. I had seen *Man of La Mancha* and thought—being young and already undone at the heart—at least now I know what love is. Ben played piano in the entry hall: a dim light, a swivel stool, no songbook. Night-watcher, he suffered from loneliness, disguised as insomnia.

"Where have you been?" he asked, not looking up, his fingers stretching for a distant note.

"I went to a play. It was wonderful," I said, and then, hesitating—"My parents took me"—so he would know it had not been a date.

"What was the play?"

"*Man of La Mancha*." I stood awkwardly, toes inverted in my tall shoes, purse strap slipping down from my shoulder.

He glanced up without smiling, and as I moved toward my door, he pulled me back again, his invisible white cane twining my neck, tensing my bones. His fingers roved the ivory for a melody.

"*Dulcinea*," he said when he found it—the song I loved—and I think then he might have smiled.

≈

"Bless the fingers,
for they are as darting as fire.
Bless the little hairs of the body,
for they are softer than grass.
Bless the hips
for they are cunning beyond all other machinery.
Bless the mouth
for it is the describer.
Bless the tongue
for it is the maker of words.
Bless the eyes
for they are the gifts of the angels,
for they tell the truth.
Bless the shoulders,
for they are a strength and a shelter.
Bless the thumb
for when working it has godly grip.
Bless the feet
for their knuckles and their modesty.
Bless the spine
for it is the whole story."

My mother was sleeping in the motel bed, a blue din of television in the background. "Let's go to the beach," my father said, tossing me a towel and some shoes. Outside in the August air, the sun descended on our shoulders like a dark gold wave. I shivered at the suddenness of it, the way warm is still cold until you get used to it.

In Seaside, Oregon, there is a small aquarium. Every season my father took me there, bought three sandwich bags full of bloody fish heads, and held me up to feed the seals. It did not seem a violence to me then, the way one takes nourishment at the expense of another. We stood behind the cyclone fence, my head pressed to the soft flesh of him, the mollusk-meat of his stomach between two shells.

"Go ahead," he said, "they are hungry."

≈

When the roses came, red as pomegranate stains, you had written a quote from Proust and forgotten to sign your name:

"It comes so soon, that moment when there is nothing left to wait for."

≈

The clock did not stop. Its hands showed no mercy, no reverence at all. I walked to the window, eyes stinging, sun so full in the sky. One of the gardeners threw down his gloves; another tripped over his pail. I thought of Lot's wife, how she had been ordered not to turn back; of Adam, who surely regretted the fruit. From the long hall to the atrium, the sun-pierced aquarium: we stood in silence, breaths we could not take in. Two men lay bleeding below us. On the pavement a black gun. Around it a puddle of blood.

*Who shoots a man in broad daylight?*
*Who shoots a man at a Christian school?*
*Who shoots a man and takes his own life?*
*WHO SHOOTS A MAN?*

I meant not to watch. I meant not to know or to feel. But there he was, right below me: this stranger, this father, this bleached seal baking in sun. They had torn his white shirt; they had torn his khaki pants. I watched him, this neutral man, this minute man (here one minute, gone the next): his breath at an arm's length, his heart beginning to stop. . . .

≈

It was after kissing, after my mouth was full of honey and moonlight, and your hands had been everywhere, touching everything there was to know about me (or so, at that moment, I thought)—

A question, like birds battering wings or long hair snarled with wind—

"Do you love me?" I wanted to know.

Your lips a syringe, a thin needle stitching:

"Maybe. *Maybe*," you said.

≈

In Wales, my one trip abroad, I came to a field studded with sheep. From a distance they resembled dandelion seeds, each fat puff on its four-legged stem. And as I approached them, their full furry bodies thickened with snow, the white-layered-white of their coats, my joy was mounting. The sheep looked up, startled at first, ears twitching quiet annoyance. *Who was this girl, all billowing hair and silly beret, all black boots and dark-breasted sweater? Why was she running, her face in a flush, her winter-cracked hands, her red fingers reaching toward them?*

≈

"Tell me a story," my lover says.

We are lying in bed, bodies paratactic and pillows propping our heads: a long, smooth symmetry of limbs. The candles have since burnt out. We are comfortable here in the dark.

*Tell me a story.*

"When I was a child, my father took me to Seaside every summer. There was an aquarium there, and in a corner of the place, hardly visible among the dark glass and sparks of swimming silver, a small sign pointed to the TOUCH TANK. It was my favorite place on earth, I think, as I mounted the little stone steps and stood, my sleeves dangling, my father rolling them up from behind, shifting his large frame and bending, a sturdy tree, toward me. I plunged in my hands. They were fast and darting as minnows, but he held them still and told me—firmly, again—these were living creatures I needed to handle with care.

Gently, then, I lifted the purple starfish, and the blazing orange, the textured bone of their bodies and those that were smooth as stone. I touched urchins with grassy spikes and snails withdrawn in shells. But the most beautiful one—where my hands lingered longest, my fingers unwilling to leave—was the soft, pulpy-pink sea anemone . . . so shy, yet she took me into her mouth, clasping the tip of my skin like a hungry wave sweeping up sand. What was I to her, she who could only feel?"

I smile, and hearing my lips split, she presses her mouth to mine. I have told nothing: no stories, no lie. *Is supplication useful?*

Now her body leans like a willow, the wave of her tongue descends.

"Kiss me," she says. "Kiss me again."

≈

I have been forty minutes in the waiting room. A woman in blue scrubs with clipboard is quietly saying my name. "Walk this way," she instructs, and I follow. The squeak of her sneakers is fear.

They come from all over, descending, zombie-like in their lab coats and fixed professional smiles. They talk around me, across me, above me. Everyone touches my throat.

"Can you feel it?" Dr. One inquires.

"Yes, right lobe, slightly protruding," the second doctor replies.

"The nodule is here," another insists. With his black magic marker he circles the place. The three men confer and then leave.

Now a woman comes. She is young and bright-faced. Her hands spell legends of pain. "We'll do our best to make you comfortable," she says, fluffing a pillow and patting a space on the long, narrow plank of a board.

"I'm going to ask you to lie down and unbutton the top of your blouse. Put your head back and tilt your neck up toward the camera. Each picture takes about five minutes during which time you must remain absolutely still. There will be one-minute breaks between pictures during which time you may relax but must remain in a horizontal position. The bed will be raised five feet off the ground, and you will slide through into the center of the machine. Please keep your hands close to your body, palms pressed inward against your thighs. This is to ensure your safety throughout the duration of the test. Do you have any questions?"

I shake my head and lay down. They could have called it *coffin, casket, crematory stove.* They could have called it anything but *bed.*

≈

The trees are shaking their leaves like salt and pepper: bright sky, clear and rippling with sun. I study the gun in my father's hand, the way he brandishes, aims, and fires.

"Like this," he says, and I draw my own pistol from the holster at my hip. I point at a tree, the sky, the sun. When I pull the trigger, I hear the loud snap of the cap and smell an invisible fire.

"Thatta girl!" my father shouts, delighted with my progress. "When I was a kid in Montana, we played Cops and Robbers all the time—Cowboys and Indians, too." Then he turns to me, eyes beaming, his own gun stuffed in his waistband, fingers loose at his sides.

A joke, familiar to me by now: "Wanna see the fastest draw in the West? Wanna see it again?"

He laughs proudly. His fingers haven't moved.

≈

One night you went out, and I wondered where you had gone. When you returned, you carried a brown paper bag and placed it under my side of the bed. "In the morning," you said. "In the morning, you may open it."

The morning was my birthday.

Twenty-three years old: my fingers still giddy to open, unwrap. I part the clenched lips of the bag. I plunge in my hands. *I am far too tired of waiting.*

"I remembered," you said, "that night you told me the story. Sister Rosemary and the Christmas party . . . I know you are always hungry."

≈

When I was twenty, my double decade sagging like a droopy lapel pin, I begged my parents, "Please, just send me away." In England and Wales, all winter, I listened to the cold speak, the frost murmuring from eves and overhangs, tracing its voice like a shimmering snake through grass.

I spent the spring near Cambridge, reading all night, too tired to sleep and soothing my hungers with tea. I had little money but plenty of time and dawdled my way around town.

There is a museum there called Kettle's Yard. A sign warns MODERN ART by the door. I went inside—a sprawling room, deliberately stark; exhibits clung to the walls. Drawn to corners, I stepped to the side, the glare of paint and paper blinding my eyes. A sign read "White Noise: Listen Closely." I stood still. I listened. I waited for something to speak.

The wall was slathered with words, thin sheets pierced with clear pins, a nexus of letters like vines. They said nothing, but as I studied and stared, I heard the pages flutter as wings, the draft of the door like a sigh. It was snowing there, in the late spring, or maybe it was rain. I felt the air heavy, suddenly, its weight on my shoulder like two white hands. . . .

*Mannequins, the wax of their skin, posing beside them in the Bon Marche window; tissue paper from the last present I opened; the crinkle of a hospital gown; candles, burning, burning down to opaque puddles in a votive cup; communion wafers in my open, my closing hand; terry-cloth towels after swimming, warm from the dryer and wrapped at the waist; an opal ring my mother wore; the lamb's-wool sweater I bought for her she kept hidden in the bottom drawer . . . .*

And I don't know how this is possible, but then, even before I knew you, I felt your fingers, the porcelain lip of the tub, your white hands washing my skin.

"Here, quick, it's hot." You hand me my latte in a paper cup. I roll down the window. Steam rises out of the car.

I sense the smooth rhythms of your body, head rolling loose on your shoulders, feet shifting pedals in turn. I feel safe here; I feel good. You turn on the radio.

*It begins with a bee sting.*

The pain returns. Five years since the first time—still, again, it takes me by surprise. You pull over to the side of the road. I uncoil my fist in your hand. Somewhere another bee is dying. I think of it in momentary elegy.

"It's OK," you say, but the stinger's still in, pin that is piercing my palm. Gently, your voice low, eyes fixed, you lift out the needle, a nettle of pain.

≈

*If you had kissed me then, I'm certain my heart would have stopped.*

# Meditation 26

*For Linda Ann Wade and Andrea Campbell: both of you, gone too soon.*

*First.*

> *If I should die before I wake,*
> *I pray the Lord my soul to take.*

I remember childhood as a slow incision across the throat: a stencil, a scalpel, a scar. Years later, when the surgeons slit and split to cut my thyroid out—that faulty organ, fickle as a heart—I trembled more from reminiscence than from fear. "Count back from twenty," they told me, chorus of masked figures in a shrinking room, and I watched the numbers falling off like years, throwback to bewilderment and darkness.

"Lights out!" my father's voice proclaims, cheerful as he guides me down the hall.

I am four again, or maybe five, and I can smell the cut grass clippings and the lazy heat of summer in the air. He leaves the window open but still draws down the shade. White fringe like the surrey with the fringe on top.

And I want to sing "OKLAHOMA!" one more time, but my father has the yard to tend, and my mother already is calling for his aid.

It is just windy enough that the weathervane on the rooftop spins in circles. I can hear the creaking horse and carriage, picture them: those bold black letters, the ones my father says spell out our family name.

Kneeling down in my night dress, I learn I am old enough to say my prayers alone. Late-evening light seeps in between the fringe and flutter of the shade.

Outside in the garden: my parents calling to each other across camellia bushes; the occasional car passing, slowing, turning down a long symmetrical drive lined with roses; neighbors greeting each other over rhododendrons and azaleas, each voice with its warm, if regimented, way.

*Now I lay me down to sleep.*

But I don't want to sleep. The whole world buzzes beyond me—beckons. "Linda, hand me the trowel!" "Have you weeded that patch of clover?" "Hi, Bill, how are you?" Why should I have to sleep before the lights go out for real, before the fat round sun sinks behind the mountains?

I try again. *Now I lay me down to sleep.*

I wonder then about summer—why it doesn't last longer, and why we have to pull up dandelions from the parking strip, and why my mother scolds if she catches me blowing those white puffs of seed. What does it mean that flowers *die* in winter, and when they come back in spring, are they the same flowers, gone down in the ground to hibernate awhile, like bears in the caves of my picture books or hidden away at Woodland Park Zoo?

*I pray the Lord my soul to keep. If I should die—*

Suddenly, I feel it: sharp needle prick of my first subjunctive: not just the flowers now, short-lived purple crocuses pushing up through the soil, fleeting tulips interspersed yellow and red along the hedge. Not just flowers, but *me*. I Might Die. I might close my eyes and never open them again. All at once I *know* this, and the knowledge itself is a kind of death: not the *might* or the *how* or the *when*, but suddenly this *will*. Startling new revelation: I WILL DIE.

"You have your whole life ahead of you," my father always said. But life, like the cold food we kept in the refrigerator—milk and eggs and cheese—was *perishable*. I didn't know the word then, but I didn't need to. Life was something that expired, that grew green fuzzy mold and turned sour. There was an end to this, to all of this: longest imaginable sleep, and still longer.

I sat on the bed, heart thumping in my neck and ears, knees drawn up beneath my chin. "Are we done now, Linda?" "Turn on the sprinklers." "Hi, Bill, how are you?" Watching, waiting. Filled with inexplicable dread. I sat there on my childhood bed, shivering despite the heat, thinking for the first time of a future. What if *tomorrow* didn't come? What did *happily ever after* really mean? So abrupt, so conspicuous a truth: time runs out, stops, ends. My head throbbed from thinking these things. The hourglass timer on the kitchen stove. Four seasons, perennially switching, forever in flux. Wilted flowers and vanishing bears. My first gloaming, alone in the gleam: just waiting for the lights to go out.

*Last.*

> One of us will die before the other.
> But we're alive now.

You've always liked that movie, *The Vanishing*. Kiefer Sutherland, Sandra Bullock, set in Washington State no less—where we first met. There he is, that Seattle man, the kind of average, understated style we'd come to admire: flannel shirt, rugged truck, arguing with his girlfriend in a gas station parking lot. All this so ordinary, so commonplace: drives and feuds and pulling over for a coffee and a quick fill-'er-up. I think of our road trips, those forty-two states, stories we told, kisses, and squabbles. But then she's gone, without a trace, and the man is haunted by a memory he can't escape. What happened to her—this woman he loved—and its corollary, that gaping wound: Does she still *exist*? Is she still *alive*? What are the chances he'll find her, befuddled but breathing somewhere?

I recall how, growing up, my mother often mourned: "I don't want anything to ever happen to you." *Anything. Ever.* We have not spoken for several years. You might say our time has run out: furious glissando and glistening keys, damper pedal slowly relieved. But sometimes I hear her voice in my head: "Stay close!" "Wake up!" "Don't stray from the path—don't you dare!"

He loved her, but he was angry. Moods shift; tensions are temporary. He never imagined he would never see her again. (That double negative.) She never dreamed she would never wake up. (Ditto.) Death, a series of dramatic ironies: my nails bitten down to the nubs, blue screen light—our plaintive helplessness watching the plot play out.

I recall also how my father would say: "Don't let the sun go down upon your anger." His intercessions on my mother's behalf: "Tell her you're sorry; you didn't mean it; you won't let it happen again." How he loved me, in spite of myself. How I was angry: Little Red with her purloined hood, streak of vagrancy she couldn't seem to quell. Time running out *like sands through the hourglass,* and the wolves and the woods and that one unmistakable path.

Death: the ultimate abduction.

Understand now how far I have come, how deep into the woods I have wandered. Does it strike you as strange, the similarity between these two sounds: *wonder* and *wander*? Both at once: no longer the *might* or the *how* or the *when*, but the *must* and the *since* and the *now*. Such relentless love—that does not preclude anger, or boast itself wise, yet humbles itself (still) before sorrow.

The man's loss is not only tangible—her body misplaced, her presence absent—but also involves an abducted knowing and a theft of hypothetical time. *They had their whole lives ahead of them,* for making up and breaking down and sliding sticky-legged into diner booths and bare-bodied into bed. But how long is life, and who truly knows when it is over? When it will be? The ghost that haunts him now is this amnesia—of never-witnessed, of phantom-happened, of didn't—couldn't—ever-see-it-coming.

Each moment: a near-death experience. Each separation: rehearsal for the Grand Finale.

I feel my mother's words rise up in my throat: *I don't want anything to ever happen to you.* But I do! I want everything good and nothing bad and the two of us together forever.

"So junior high," you sigh.

"I won't be done," I tell you stubbornly, thinking of our future that culminates somewhere, of that cul-de-sac with one of us left lonely, stopped in her tracks, *derailed,* yet expected (in time) to turn around.

Sad sex isn't sexy, and fear-of-death sex is just so hard to explain—touching again what you're already missing, feeling it slip (over and over) through your clumsy, butter-slick hands.

I think of us, deep in the Arkansas dark, the hostile pursuit of strangers. Or the bright morning near Bridgeport, Connecticut: tires screeching, synapse of wind, our small car sandwiched between two larger. My arm's reflexive snap toward your shoulder as the force of impact lurched our bodies forward.

And then in the Denver predawn, waiting at the rest stop while you and a high school band marched solemnly toward the single row of stalls. It was all I could do not to rush in after you, peer under each stall for your shoes.

Afterward, when I saw you walking toward me, wavy hair drawn back in a ponytail, black T-shirt and fading blue jeans; when I surveyed the bliss of your body, the slender limbs and pectin-sweet skin and darting blue eyes swift as minnows; when I smiled and you smiled back and some secret knowledge passed between us with the ease of precedent and the promise of surprise; and then the sun flared up behind you, torrent of light suddenly blinding my eyes, I felt the desperation slacken, the fear recede. Thinking first: your bony arches and acrobatic toes. Thinking next: your long fingers, bearing no resemblance to mine. And then: the soft flutter of your mouth, your smooth shadow's cast of morning shade. *All those deaths I've crossed on straw.* The man, spinning circles. The woman, chloroformed unconscious. That brambled, misaligned path, brimming with traps and scratches.

Or maybe I was thinking none of these things. Hungry for eggs over easy and a coffeepot perched on our table. Caffeine-deprived. Dirty. Lust-ridden and dusty from the all-night drive. But I saw it clear, *shot through the heart*, as the tape deck loudly proclaimed. Bon Jovi knew as well as we did: how perishable we were, how precious. . .

*Subsequent.*

> *Because life, however we live it, is unbelievable.*

Before I was born, my grandfather went into the hospital and never came out. By all accounts, he simply disappeared. I don't know the season or the precise hour of the day, but somewhere in Seattle in 1971, John Campbell Wade—a tall, lanky, traveling Goodyear salesman, an asthmatic, comic, father of two, pipe smoker, lover of llamas and libraries and fresh-squeezed orange juice with fried wiener and mustard sandwiches on white crustless bread—died from accumulated fluid in the lungs. Quietly, in his sleep, he drowned.

John was alone, believing he had come to be treated for a bad cough, one of his recurrent "spells." He had quit smoking again, and with his children grown, there were no longer animals in the home to aggravate his condition. When my grandmother returned the next morning—I can see her with taupe purse and tight curls, stockings loose at her ankles and a freshly pressed dress—his bed was empty, stripped down to the white mattress pad. She had come to pick him up, take him home, prop him with pillows in front of the television set. Life would go on as usual: Sunday drives along Alki Beach, bridge nights with the neighbors, Bill and his new wife coming over for dinner, their daughter Linda with her endless string of beaus. Instead, a nurse intercepted, said they had tried to call. "He was peaceful," she explained, touching my grandmother's hand. "We tried, but we couldn't save him."

At sixty years old, my grandmother became a widow. She has been so for thirty-five years. (Longer, I note, than the length of her marriage.) She wears her thin wedding band and signs her checks "Mrs. John Wade." In her mind, she is still married. Death has not parted them at all.

"Where is my grandfather?" I asked her once: seven years old, an ardent student of UNO.

"He's all around us," my grandmother said, discarding a blue two. "If you talk to him, I believe he can hear you."

"Like God?"

She smiled, flashing her improbably white teeth rimmed with gold. "Well, not quite like God, but he's *with* God, and he can listen, even though he can't answer your prayers."

That night, alone in my room, I try it. I say: "Hello, Grandpa. You don't know me exactly, but I hope you know I was born. I'm Bill's daughter. I want a cat. More than anything in the whole world. I'd like a tabby cat like the one I saw at the pet store, and if I had her, I'd call her Mango, and she'd follow me everywhere. Aunt Linda says you were really allergic to animal hair, but you still let her have a kitten named Sparky. And she told me about the little duck she saved at the pond and how you let her keep him too until he got so big she had to take him to her friend who lived on a farm. Grandma says I can't ask you for presents because you're not God or Santa Claus, but I would like it if you could help me find a cat that needs a home. I'd take really good care of him, I promise."

It's a wild card, which means you can play any color. I put down a green eleven. Only two cards left. I'm anxious to win.

"Do you get lonely?" I ask Grandma June. "This is a pretty big house for just one person."

"How could I get lonely when I have you to visit me? And then Aunt Linda comes and stays over on the weekends."

"UNO!" I squeal, waving my single card in anticipated triumph.

"Guess I'll have to do something about that," and with a stroke of her hand, her new card commands me: *Draw 2.*

"My daddy always lets me win," I sigh.

"Wouldn't you rather win on your own?"

"I guess so."

Then, she offers to make me a fried wiener and mustard sandwich on Wonder bread. She knows how I love the bag with the red, yellow, and blue balloons.

"Tell me more about my grandfather, like the time when he gave a Cloret to a llama at the zoo because his breath was bad, or the time he rolled down the window and mooed at all the cows until they came running over to the roadside."

"You know those stories," my grandmother says, pouring me a glass of orange juice.

Because I am young, my candor comes easier, poses less of a threat: "Is it harder"—I want to know—"loving someone after he's dead?"

*Please, Grandpa, I want a cat so bad!*

Finding those pipes in my father's office, set back on the bookshelf, hidden from view. I have just read a Nancy Drew book about a secret switch that makes a bookcase swing open: behind it, a set of mystery stairs. My father's bookcase doesn't have that switch, though I have spent hours searching. Instead, there are these pipes, and I clutch them each in my teeth the way sophisticated men with neck scarves and pocket watches always seem to do in old-time movies. They taste bad, and I don't have any matches. Still, I keep one, hoping to smoke it someday. Hoping to conjure this man I have never met.

. . .

"If *uno* means one in Spanish, what is two?"

"*Dos*," my grandma replies.

"Do you know everything?"

Sipping her coffee: "Not *everything*."

"So when Grandpa was alive, you were *dos*, but now that he's gone, you're *uno*."

Her pale blue eyes regard me softly. "That's one way of looking at it."

"Did you tell me that Grandpa used to work for Goodyear?"

"Yes, he did. He sold tires. He drove all over the country."

"My daddy says he even drove in snowstorms."

"Yes, he did. Many times. He was a good driver. I always felt safe with Johnny."

And I want to tell her about my new cat, who was a stray and whom my parents finally consented I could keep. Mittens, who has little white feet and a white scrawny belly but a shiny black coat, and though he's shy and still skittish around strangers, he lives in a box on our back porch and eats tuna right out of the can. My dad says he'll get fatter and less afraid. *Give him time.*

But the real story isn't that I found Mittens. It's that I think my grandfather helped me find him, and I am keeping all to myself the secret clue. That morning in October, when the hungry kitten crouched and whimpered, curled inside the hedge-growth of a local park—when I heard him mewing and tucked him into my coat and carried him home, believing beyond all doubts that he was the cat I was meant to have—something amazing happened. I saw the Goodyear blimp floating above me, and I don't know what purpose a blimp actually serves, but I felt certain my grandfather was aboard it. In the little basket dangling below, I imagined him—his black Brylcreemed hair, his Coke-bottle glasses—waving to me, urging me on.

"UNO!" my grandma exclaims, and I watch her, happy, laying her last card down.

*Penultimate.*

> *The longing is to be pure.*
> *What you get is to be changed.*

In the mine in Wales, we descend dozens of feet into the ground. Our guide curses Margaret Thatcher and his lost livelihood. I notice how the air thins, chills, accompanied by unexpected clarity. Life seems simpler underground, all the detritus having risen to the surface.

"Let's stop here," the guide decides. Twenty college students stand behind him: awkward, slouched, American.

He turns and paces in front of us, studying our faces as though there will be a quiz following. Pausing in front of me, the weathered man in clunky work boots and enormous fur-lined gloves announces his purpose: "On the count of three, we are all going to turn off our lights and experience absolute darkness." I bite my lip. "The darkest darkness there is." He chuckles loudly. "Darker than death."

This will be no cinematic dark, no migraine night with all the curtains drawn and beach towels blocking vagrant shafts of light. I'm envisioning some Agatha Christie twist where one of us disappears before the lights flash back, phantom victim of an unseen crime. I bite my lip again till I taste blood.

He counts, and we obey, and a moment later—visor lights extinguished in unison—our row of silent tourists exhales into disbelief. Too dark for shadows, and the air is light and strangely clean, and I want to hold on to what it feels like: the closest I have ever been to disembodied. It's brighter, I find, under my eyelids, where I can watch the scratchy picture show of what I still know, re-member, and imagine. But when I open my eyes, the hollow dark lingers and surrounds. Is this death: sneak preview of a coming attraction? What of the tunnel survivors attest ends in light?

When we emerge above ground, I touch my cheeks. They are wet with tears I don't remember crying.

I begin to think about death as a kind of estrangement, not only from life and from those we love who are living but also from whole ways of life. In Europe, I remain celibate, virginal, guarding my body as if it were a safe. (It feels more like a tomb.) I watch the other girls shed weighty clothes of sobriety, propriety, suffer the slings and arrows of outrageous flings and cross-national romances. Is something wrong with me that I don't feel the way I'm supposed to? Will I always appear in pantomime, simply going through the motions? During strained weekly conversations with my parents, they ask if I'm "meeting people, going out, making the most of everything."

"I guess so," I tell them, knowing they didn't want me here to begin with, that they keep a poster-sized calendar on an easel in their living room, marking off the days till I return. "I *have* been to a lot of museums . . . "

But museums are about death also. Relics. Remnants. Scraps. What's the difference after all between a gallery and a graveyard—places you go to pay homage to the past?

My roommate is a pleasant, social girl. I have no reason not to like her, yet I feel strangely unsettled by our interactions. Twin beds. Late nights. Close quarters. Tina has a boyfriend at home in the States who sends her roses on Valentine's Day, a crate of Florida oranges when he travels to Jacksonville. Her life is shaping up nicely. She belongs to a sorority. She has been inducted under strict vows of normality, aesthetics.

Once, I walk in on her in the bath. She has failed to lock the door. I have failed to knock. We each assume the other is still in class in the city, nearly an hour's train ride away. What I notice is not her body, which holds no particular appeal, but the look of horror on her face—as if a calculated treason had been committed. Tina regards me suspiciously now, huddles with her friends on the platform.

At home, my best friend prepares for her wedding. I have agreed to read a sonnet on her behalf. My parents will be there, commending her for doing "the right thing," entering into this virtuous enterprise called marriage. I will recruit boyfriends to diminish the glow of the halo of suspicion that seems now to perpetually adorn my head. Sex will become the secret switch to the bookcase of my body, but no one will find the mystery stairs.

What I mistake for the growing numbness that estranges me from others is not in fact some dire complicity but an uprising taking place underground. In the graceful dark, I run unfamiliar streets, admiring the houses in which I do not live, the families to which I do not belong. I begin to know myself as *not like the others*, despite how hard I've tried, despite my fiancé and intended pas de deux as wife and mother. For a few months: this recurring dream of meeting friends who are instead chalk outlines of bodies.

Noting the road sign on the cul-de-sac: *Dead End.* Running past it and farther and harder until I stop suddenly in my tracks. *Derailed*? Lonely and learning slowly to turn around.

My parents will not accept me. My fiancé will not forgive me. I know this, going in. I face this, coming out—which is also a kind of death. I tell myself it is only Angie and loving her so much: the one person in all the world I could imagine being stuck with at the top of the Ferris wheel. Or back in time together: a glass capsule—teardrop of light—at the center of the London Eye.

*Rising.*

> *Any man's death diminishes me because I am involved with mankind.*

Unlike my grandfather, whom I never met and was therefore free to imagine—even to love—without the hindrance imposed by memory or mourning, Rick Brown was the first person I ever knew who actually died. Here today, gone tomorrow . . . Now you see him, now you don't . . . Houdini stunt taken to new levels.

I knew Rick Brown because I played tennis and Nintendo with his daughter and because my mother played Bingo with his wife and because he lived down the street from us and always worked out in his yard the way my own father did, pushing his manual lawnmower. Each day we drove home from school, my father leaned out the window and waved, honking his horn as we passed.

But Rick and Judy had been fighting. Even Kristy mentioned they hadn't been getting along. And a man in a dark blue suit, dressed as if for a wake, arrived at their house one late afternoon with divorce papers sealed in hand.

"What's happening with the Browns? Place has been deserted all week."

My father fished for information, and my mother gladly tugged the line. "Judy's divorcing him. Claims a loveless marriage. Suing for everything: house, car, kids."

"On what grounds? *Loveless*? I never saw a man more devoted to his wife and family. And have you seen those Japanese maples he planted last year?"

"All I know is what Judy tells me, and she says she's never been happy with him."

Moods shift; tensions are temporary. "*Never*?"

"She says she's never loved him, and I believe her. She said she only married him because she thought she couldn't do any better."

My father sits in his big yellow chair, brooding. He calls it *reading*, but I can always tell the difference.

"You haven't turned the page for a really long time," I observe, perching on the stool by his feet.

"I'm just concentrating, that's all," he mumbles, patting my tumbleweed curls.

"Mom wanted me to remind you to wind the grandfather clock and after that, there are some pots that need watering on the patio."

"I'm tired," he sighs. "Can you help me? You're a decade now. That's practically grown," then looks up at me and smiles.

"Yeah," I tell him, "I can fill the watering can, but Mom says you have to deadhead the fuchsias."

"Why can't she do it—or you?"

"Well, she has Bingo tonight, and she thinks I can't tell the difference between new buds and dying blossoms."

"Can you?"

I study the garden from our living room window: chaos of petals, carnage of leaves. Shaking my head then, conceding: "I don't think so." Finally: "I'm not sure."

So divorce is a kind of death, and marriage also: a passing on from one state of being into another. Was there room for a U-turn? A driveway for backing up and shifting gears? I didn't think so. I wasn't sure. But I feared for my parents—their own fragile state—and for the dissolution of bonds deemed indestructible by God and a Justice of the Peace.

In the end, though, death and not divorce did part them. Rick called Judy and asked her down to their church, a quiet spot called Fenton Glen where they could talk. He was "ready to settle," he said, and he didn't want the children there. They would speak candidly, he was clear about that. "Whatever you do, don't bring the children."

"Are you sure you should go alone?" my mother inquired. "What if he's angry? What if he's seeking some kind of revenge?"

"Don't be absurd. Rick would never *hurt* me. The worst he'll do is try to win me back."

Then she was off, her horrible heels clicking, and her scent of thick perfume wafting through the room—that ominous cloud.

*Little did she know.*

Little did anyone know, never would anyone have imagined, that earlier that afternoon Rick Brown, wearing his signature flannel shirt, driving his old rugged truck that he used to transport yard debris to the dump, had hung himself up with a sturdy rope from an oak tree overlooking Fenton Glen. There, beside the Fauntleroy Creek and the Fauntleroy Community Church, above the bench where young lovers kissed and touched under the stray foliage passing for privacy—that pastoral place, where parishioners sometimes prayed—Rick Brown ended his life forever. "A permanent solution to a temporary problem," as many were prone to say.

Shaking his head then, conceding. That chaos of petals. That carnage of leaves.

His note that read only YOU DID THIS TO ME.

And Judy the one to find him.

*Falling.*

> *Choose one word and say it over*
> *and over, till it builds a fire inside your mouth.*

In twelfth grade, that word for me was *thanatos*, meaning death drive or fatal instinct. Not the same as suicide or suicidal—more philosophical than that—but a kind of pleasure taken in the thought of dying: the pursuit of death.

At seventeen, consumed by fantasies of my own extinction, my journal evolved in obsessive thanatopsis. I collected tales of unexplained deaths, people gone missing *out of the blue*, Hemlock reports of unusual or artful demise. Afternoons, waiting for my father, I climbed the ancient stone stairs of my Catholic school, a looming melancholy structure that commanded an entire city block. Holy Names Academy, established in 1880, the premier girls' school of its time (and mine), embodied an otherworldliness that suited my skittish Protestant self—altered consciousness of heavy ritual, Latin incantation. And the music, how it soothed me: granting uselessness, blessing anonymity. Those furious glissandi, those glistening keys. . . .

On the third floor: a replica of the Sistine Chapel where we assembled for daily mass, confessionals honeycombed in corners. I found my way back to the empty pews, long after the school day had ended. I gazed up at the domed ceiling, talcum-pink and smooth as the inside of an egg, recalling what the legend professed: that years before, a tortured young priest had hung himself there, falling (as a broken-necked bird) from the high wooden rafters. Some versions claimed he had fallen in love with a nun, had given way to temptation, was shamed to death by his sin. Other versions, retold in callous tones, pronounced the dead priest gay, driven mad by homosexual desire.

I shivered to think of it: *sin*—such a bleak word—leading down that brambled, misaligned path. To where? Death? Chorus of masked figures in a shrinking room. And why celibacy? And why vows? Did God really care how we spent our bodies, who caressed them—or who we desired would? The harder question still: did God really *care*?

I thought of Nietzsche's declaration that God is dead, and I wondered whether God had ever lived—*mustn't we live to die?* Or had God in fact fallen prey to a thanatopic vanquishing: crucified not as the body of his son, but abolished instead as a universal state of mind. A given. Now we had the option not to believe, to turn Doubting Thomas, every one. My mind wandered again, affixed to a thought as though there would be a quiz following: could raw belief render anything *true*?

I knelt on the low bench with its meager cushion. I tried to remember how it felt to pray—when it used to be effortless. But in my mind, two images kept crossing: the faceless priest, dangling from a fraying rope, and Jesus, eyes upturned, nailed to an impossibly feeble cross. Sometimes the face of Jesus was the face of Rick Brown, and sometimes the priest was Arthur Dimmesdale, naked and self-mutilated, wriggling on a nascent line. I wanted to speak, to know the words for the problem of hope and the yearning for succor. Words like *quandary, conundrum.* Smaller words like *safe* and *full.*

I looked around at the stained glass windows, the predictable (now rote) positions called the Stations of the Cross. What was happening to me? How had I become so exiled from certainty, buried here (hibernating?) in the dark closet of my mind. *Darkest darkness there is.* Might I be rescued still? Or would I need, in the end, to be exhumed?

*Please, Grandpa, I want a life so bad!*

In December of that year, Mrs. Thomas, one of the young laywomen who taught physical education and health sciences, woke to find her husband cold and motionless in bed beside her. While she slept, he had risen, skulked off to the kitchen, and poisoned himself. Quietly, in his sleep, he died.

The news rippled through our high school hallways at warp speed. "Mr. Thomas killed himself!" "Did she know he was depressed?" "Was there a note at all—any explanation?"

I sat in biology class, stunned. Before me: a limp squid, the small mollusk we were required to dissect. Only two months before at the autumn tolo, I had watched Mrs. Thomas and her husband move among us as chaperones. Dancing awkwardly with a male friend, leaning into his body the way other girls did—cooing, whispering, pressing their breasts against the starched white shirts of their companions—I saw my future flashing before my eyes: how I would never be elegant, never be coy.

Mrs. Thomas wasn't elegant either. Tall the way I was, best suited to jeans and a baseball jersey, hair lifted high off her face with a natural radiance not enhanced by makeup: I studied her across my dancing partner's shoulder. At one point, her husband drew her out on the floor, under the low lights, bodies all around them bumping and humming like molecules. She smiled at him, softened under his touch. *They had their whole lives ahead of them,* for making up and breaking down. . . . I noticed how they fit together, each anticipating the other's step, gliding along to what may have been the final love song of their mutual lives.

There would be a mass, and we would march solemnly toward our assigned places in the pews. "We begin by making a small incision in the buccal mass." We would watch as the priest broke bread and blessed it, raised a chalice of wine and blessed it. "Gently peel back the flesh till you can see the stellate ganglion." We would listen as he shook the small silver bell, imagine the divine spirit descending, *transubstantiating* bread into body, wine into blood. "Spread apart the tentacles and use a probe to feel inside the mouth." We would walk forward, two by two, to receive the sacrament: that small morsel, laid to rest on the tongue. "Notice how the squid has three hearts. . . . " Mrs. Thomas leaning against the wall, her eyes downcast, not walking forward, one trembling hand across her chest. " . . . two gill hearts to force blood under pressure to the gills, and a systemic heart to force blood under pressure to the rest of the body."

She would leave suddenly, slipping through the unused cloisters into the bridal room and down the mystery stairs. Perhaps Mrs. Thomas, too, was consumed by fantasies of her own extinction. Perhaps she also struggled with prayer, or at that plaintive moment, the baser functions of breath and tears. *Thanatos.* Over and over. Building a fire inside her mouth.

What could I have done? "This is the Savior's Body, given for you." Culpability, my faithful shadow, once again stretched its tentacles toward me, peeling back my pliable flesh. "This is the Savior's Blood, shed for you."

Who can speak to Death—who is brave enough to address it?

Or Bermuda's Triangle, better known as Love, from which—should we emerge at all—we cannot be but altered.

*Fulcrum.*

> *Until the Moss had reached our lips—*
> *And covered up—our names—*

When I was a child, the walls resounded with JoAnne, her voice constant as a clock chime, her name permanent as the porch light that guided visitors into our home. My mother's best friend since junior high, JoAnne swept through the world on a patchouli cloud, her long skirts swishing, her dark eyes darting, swift as minnows. She came for Bingo and patio potlucks, always running late and juggling too many bags and stumbling over the straps of her sandals. I peeked out my bedroom door in time to catch the gleam of her smile, her generous hand waving to me, urging me on.

Have you ever noticed how the death of a woman is also the death of her name? Men flourish in posthumous prestige; their commodified monikers turn bequest or monument. Women vanish differently and more completely. And so it was with JoAnne.

In the winter, when the moles on her back turned malignant, when doctors pronounced the dreaded word—*melanoma*—everyone believed she would survive. "Such a strong spirit." "With a son to raise." "God wouldn't strike a woman in the prime of life."

But God struck all kinds of people all the time! This I knew. This much I knew. Swaddled in gray sweaters, I stared at the gray rain: bright autumnal world reduced to monochrome.

As the months wore on, my mother refused to take me with her to the hospital. She wanted me to remember JoAnne as she had been—not as the wan and docile woman she had become. Blue-complected, bald.

"But if you care for someone, if you"—hesitating—"*love* someone, shouldn't you be there? Shouldn't you go, no matter what?"

My mother shook her head firmly. "JoAnne understands. She wouldn't want you to see her this way."

Seeing was believing. My mother didn't want me to believe.

Meanwhile, a new girl sits beside me in Language Arts class. Her name is Mandie Salazar, and she wears purple lipstick and Lee Press-On Nails. Her lashes and eyelids perpetually sparkle.

Mandie struggles with diagramming sentences, so in exchange for my help, she provides complimentary manicures in her makeshift beauty shop.

"This school thing is just temporary," she tells me with twelve-year-old aplomb. "I'm going to get my GED and become a cosmetologist."

"Is that like a fortune-teller?" I ask, gazing at her through a pungent haze of Exclamation perfume.

"No, silly! It's someone who's an expert in making people beautiful." She files my nails thoughtfully. "A *world-famous* cosmetologist."

My mother finds a page of notebook paper with Mandie Salazar's name written over and over. My sleekest cursive. A heart adorning the i. A flower braided into the r. She stops me in the hallway, cryptic, unsmiling: "I'd just die if you were a lesbian." *I'd just die.*

When Mandie transfers to another school, we don't speak of her anymore. My mother regards me with suspicion now, skulks off to the hospital.

"Is JoAnne going to die?" I ask my father.

He turns to me, darkness encroaching under his eyes. It pains him to answer: "Doesn't look good."

*Please, Grandpa, don't let JoAnne die!*

Another equinox. Thick fog obscures the sun. Frost and fragile blossoms.

My mother buys me lipstick and braids my hair. "Why don't you like shopping like other girls do? What's *wrong* with you?"

*Please, Grandpa, bring Mandie back; bring her here!*

And one day, just like that, the walls were silent. *JoAnne* no longer bandied about, no longer echoed. A horrible, deep hush had fallen. My mother, dressed in black, drove me to school. I read the sign as we passed by: "Holy Rosary. Funeral Mass Today. 10 AM."

Lips taut. Fingers pinched. *All those deaths I've crossed on straw.*

I remember childhood as a slow incision across the throat: a stencil, a scalpel, a scar. This moment, in particular. There I was, just sitting in my chair, gazing out the window of Language Arts class. The teacher, again, instructing me to pay attention. The desk beside me, vacant once more. Across the street and up the steep cathedral stairs, I saw my mother, wearing a wide-brimmed hat and sunglasses to mask the glare—or the tears. Church bells chimed, hordes of mourners spilling into the street. My mother lingered on the landing. Watching, waiting. Filled with inexplicable dread.

She had lost someone who could not be replaced. Culpability, my faithful shadow . . . I felt my own self receding, my own good name lost. I knew then there were no unbreakable bonds.

My mother took off her sunglasses, wiped them dry. She stood in the gold light, facing my direction. It was then I began to raise my hand, as if to wave, as if to urge her on. But something stopped me. Something hard and unwilling in me froze. I stared through the window, cheeks wet with tears. How to say this— we saw each other, and we did not see each other.

# Bouquet

*If you are in the garden, I will dress myself in leaves . . .*
—Mary Oliver

**Love • in • a • Mist**

*(Nigella damascena) Annual garden flower. Delicate blossoms, usually blue and white. "Self-sows" readily. Once established, can be difficult to remove. Common name derives from the nestling of flowering buds in a lacy involucre.*

I have had too much wine. My cerebellum sings, and the swarm of bees rising up from my knees causes a faulty kinesthesia. *Could you excuse me, please?* The room is humming like a hot hive. I touch my temples. They are burning. The fog of my breath on the bathroom mirror makes a shape of cloud or clover.

*I'm looking over a four-leaf clover that I overlooked before.*

Is it me singing now, or Art Mooney's voice crooning through the walls of Le Chat Noir?

*One leaf is sunshine, the second is rain, third is the roses that grow in the lane. . . .* Distant and bluesy, not the way my mother played it on her baby grand.

At the table, you are waiting, drunk but more able than I. You have ordered something praline, and your lips are slick with remnants of cream. *Meringue me!* I am all mouth and no hands, fumbling for a tiny swatch of silver.

"Do you hear that?"

"Hear what?"

*No need explaining, the one remaining is somebody I adore!*

Candles flicker. Your breath has a cadence to it. Buzzing again at the back of my eyes. "Cheers, cheers, to your golden birthday."

Our glasses clink, our fingers jostle. *If I could, I would swallow you whole.*

### Cornflower

*(Centaurea cyanus) Also known as Bachelor's button, which refers to the long-lasting quality of the flower when cut and placed in the buttonhole of a shirt or suit. Decades ago, bachelors sported the flower when they went courting. These dark blue flowers grow wild in cornfields and bloom until the harvest begins.*

There is no question life was simpler with a man. *Simple*, I say, not *easy*. Whenever an established precept came into doubt (who would wash the dishes, who would argue with the paperboy)—whenever one facet of our humanity chafed or challenged the other's, leaving a fresh choice to be made—we fell back into our genders like warm blankets. Many sentences began, "After all, he is the man," and many others, "How typical of her, being a woman."

Pronouns puzzle me as even such small words are weighted differently. When I hear or speak them, I notice this discrepancy: the heavy-stone hiss of *his*, commandment masquerading as adjective; and *her*, feather-light and flexible, just trifling, not wanting to impose. I remember a campfire tale about a man who froze to death in the forest because his wife had sewn tiny magnets inside his mittens, and over time the magnets altered the arrows on his compass so they no longer provided an accurate reading. He had no idea where he was going, so he just walked in circles till he died.

At one time, I longed to be the second in a fresh set of towels: *his 'n' hers*, with the glossy gold cursive and the monogram: a letter I would not recognize and could only claim by proxy: Mrs. Fill-in-the-Blank, as if I were missing an ingredient or had been assembled incomplete.

On an interview: *List three adjectives that best describe you.* Messy, elusive, snarled.

Did I lie? Did I misrepresent myself? Warning: certainties not included. Small print: hoping no one would notice.

But when I met you, the story does not turn fairy tale. The wanderer in the forest does not stumble upon a gingerbread house, only to open the door and find a sensual Wiccan waiting to shampoo her hair and bring her to climax in front of the fire. No rose petals and bearskin rug. No felicity with figs and feathers.

Instead: each year when the spring comes, I line my collar with little blue flowers and ask again, with foreknowledge and flush, *will you please come outside and walk around in circles with me?*

## Amaryllis

*(Also Hippeastrum) Meaning "splendid beauty" or "pride," Amaryllis was a popular woman's name in ancient Greece. The petals are known to be flamboyantly red and will flower after two years of culture.*

Time is what there is never enough of. But Sappho says, and I believe her—*The moon rose full, and as around an altar, stood the women.*

It would be false to say: *it is your woman-ness I love, and this only.*

It would be false to say: *it is your human-ness I love, and this only, regardless of sex, irrespective of gender.*

What is true is that I have loved you longer than three years now. There is no foreseeable finish to the heart's interminable project, and only rough proof of such elaborate geometry.

## Queen Anne's Lace

*Prolific wildflower. Can be found growing untended along roadsides and in fields almost anywhere in America. Left fallow, its seeds quickly spread.*

"You're in the South now, and in the South, it's called chiggerweed."

From the car window, you gesture to the frilly weed-flowers skirting the road, gathered in small colonies as if to protect themselves from invasion. Safety, always, in numbers.

"Why chiggerweed?" I repeat.

"Because the heads of the flowers are full of them. Chiggers, I mean. Talk about a breeding ground . . ."

We have driven seven days to see your family, my first venture over the

Mason-Dixon line. And now, in the hard heat of the Tennessee summer, I feel a shiver coming on. *Please, let them like me, please . . .*

"There are some rich people over in Brentwood who wanted Queen Anne's Lace for their wedding. They paid a lot of money to have it *brought in* from more rural places." Your lips curling, your eyebrows raised. "And we were all just laughing, thinking how silly they were. Out here you pay people to have your weeds removed, or you leave well enough alone; that's more likely."

Irony, our mutual friend—yet I can't resist:

"Maybe sometimes beauty's enough." (Your eyes rolling now.) "Maybe, for the flowers' sake, the chiggers are worth it."

## Moonflower and Morning Glory

*(Ipomoea alba and Ipomoea tricolor) Moonflowers open in the evenings so they can be pollinated by night-flying moths. Their white complexion attracts moths, and they emit a sweet and not-too-potent fragrance. The moonflower is a close relative of the morning glory, which opens in the morning so it can be pollinated by bees and other insects active during the day.*

We are perfect opposites, you and I. How in the evenings, as night descends softly over the day, casting its wild and prodigious shadows, you come alive inside. Your eyes dilate like cats' eyes in darkness: bright, attentive. Your second wind a breath blowing all through the house, rousing the ferns, ruffling the curtains. I fall asleep in your arms, recede to where it is safe: pillow of your solar plexus.

Then, morning: what the proverbs call *wiser than the eve*. But it isn't wisdom we're talking about. It's the way our bodies bend toward the light, sun or moon, warm or cool, and blossom each in their separate times. I hold you close to me in the wreckage of our bed—the cast-off covers and scattered clothes—and allow myself the privilege of your face. Those eyelashes long as harp strings, the quiver of your mouth against a dream.

How can it be, two flowers of the same species, the distinctness of their geotropic designs?

*Describe in one sentence the person you love.*

She holds me when I fall asleep in the evening; I hold her till she awakens in the dawn.

**Love • Lies • Bleeding**

*(Amaranthus) The entire gesture of Love-Lies-Bleeding is downward, each plant forming sweeping arches that embrace the Earth. The color of the plant is vibrant, with magenta and red infusing the stems and seeds. The "bleeding out" of the Amaranthus relates to its healing quality. Love-Lies-Bleeding has proven to be a powerful balm for those undergoing great physical and psychic pain.*

When I thought for the first time I would lose you, everything stopped. Every muscle in my body coiled. They mentioned "surgery," "treatments," and "health care costs," but all I could hear was "death." *Death*, like the distant chill of a post-hypnotic suggestion. How that word followed me, crouched and hovered, threatening to bring you harm.

It doesn't matter that in the end it was all "a terrible mistake," that they had "overestimated the extent of the problem." The damage was done. Some great and necessary illusion had been shattered. What mattered was not that I would have given my life for you, every last drop of my veins. I knew that already; I understood going in. But this notion that there might be nothing I could do— no cell to harvest, no skin to graft—that I would be asked to do the unthinkable: to surrender a life that was not my own and without which my own life could not continue.

"Such melodrama," you sigh, but I am not lying. When death comes for you in his carriage—may it be years from now—I will have my own suitcases waiting, affairs arranged. He must also stop—kindly—for me.

**Mistletoe**

*Evergreen parasitic plant, growing on the branches of trees, where it forms pendent bushes, two to five feet in diameter. It grows and has been found on almost any deciduous tree, preferring those with soft bark, and being, perhaps, most common on old apple trees, though it is frequently found on the ash, hawthorn, lime, and other trees. On the oak, it grows very seldom. Mistletoe is a true parasite, for at no period does it derive nourishment from the soil, or from decayed bark, like some fungi do. All nourishment is obtained from its host. The roots become woody and thick.*

Yes, I was always a romantic. In college, with my first boyfriend in Eugene, Oregon: how we spent hours driving around, searching for the perfect tree. "It has to be an oak," I remember saying, though I have since learned that mistletoe on oak trees is less than likely. So we were chasing in part a myth and also in part a wish: that we would be happy together; that our search would be finished before it had even begun.

At last, in the parking lot of a Presbyterian church, we watched as a magisterial oak trembled in the throes of a storm: branches broken off and strewn across the windshield of his father's newly polished car. When the wind had lessened and the world stood still, we stepped out to admire the damage. And there, still clinging to the lower limbs of the tree, was mistletoe—live mistletoe with its lovely berries—and I climbed up desperate to reach it.

What a triumph it was, kissing him in his father's car with my arms full of mistletoe and still more scattered across the dash. They were, for that moment, the best kisses of my life because, in my young logic, I believed somehow I had *earned* them.

But you I have kissed hundreds of times, more than any other human alive. Not once under the mistletoe. Spontaneous kisses, sleepy kisses, just-waking-up kisses and joyous-celebration kisses. I have kissed you to cure hiccups (yours and mine), kissed you in the midst of a laugh and a yawn. I have kissed you salty at the seashore, sticky in the rain, in every season, night or day, in forty-two states of this country, the District of Columbia, and Canada.

Not one was earned, required, or deserved. Yet each kiss *a kiss to build a dream on* . . .

**September Flower**

*(Aster dumosus and Aster novae-angliae) Mostly perennials, a few are annuals and biennials. All have alternate simple leaves that are untoothed or toothed but rarely lobed. In late summer and autumn, the asters produce large clusters of flowering heads, although a few species have single heads. Each head contains a central disk of small yellow (sometimes orange, purple, or white) tubular flowers surrounded by numerous showy ray flowers ranging from blue or violet shades of purple, to red, pink, or white. The ray flowers are never yellow. The tubular flowers are bisexual, having both a pistil and stamens; the ray flowers are usually sterile.*

For many years, I had a friend I loved. She was quiet, pensive, a writer of substance and insight. We lived together in college, and upon my return from six months abroad, she asked me to give a reading and blessing at her wedding. I remember the words I spoke, borrowed from Shakespeare at her request: *Let me not to the marriage of true minds admit impediments.*

Maybe she was young and making a mistake. Maybe she was afraid, having never been with any other man and fearing no other would love her as well. I did not judge. I did not admit impediments but raised my glass in celebration.

*Love is not love which alters when it alteration finds, or bends with the remover to remove.*

Sometimes we all foolishly believe that what we seek and crave and occasionally discover is desirable for everyone, or worse: that we are the best doctors to prescribe such happiness for others. I lived the next two years emulating what my friend had done—searching for the husband who would love me above all others, whose presence would assuage my doubts and grant me absolution from my perennial loneliness.

One night, in the humid gleam that is September, I called my friend and told her, "I have found love, and where I least expected. I was not looking for her, yet there she was."

*Oh, no, it is an ever-fixed mark which looks on tempests and is never shaken.*

Again, the power of the pronoun, the dread of alteration. I heard my friend's silence, terrible and tenuous, on the other end of the phone and knew at once I had stepped out on a tightrope for which there was no net.

At last: "I don't know what to say. I don't understand what's happened."

"I told you what's happened. I'm in love. Isn't it wonderful?"

"But with a *woman?*" Whispering the last word as though it had become suddenly shameful. "How is that possible? What are you . . . I mean . . . are you . . . *bisexual* now? Is that it?"

"Maybe. I guess. I hadn't really thought about it. Do you hear what I'm saying? I'm in love!"

*It is the star to every wand'ring bark, whose worth's unknown, although his height be taken.*

"You never said anything about this before. You didn't tell me you were *capable of*—"

She was crying, and in the past, I would have been the one to console. But now it was me, helpless, insisting, "What does it matter *who* I love? Why do I need a label?"

Then, my friend, the one I had trusted beyond reproach, who had trusted me the same, voiced her betrayal with a new and forceful clarity: "I don't care if you're bisexual. Everyone knows it's just code for lesbian anyway. You lead people along for a while, give them hope that maybe—"

I didn't ask what she meant. I knew what she meant. Hope that it wasn't true, that the phantom girl-crush would evaporate and, with it, the possibility of such unthinkable things.

"I *changed* in front of you." She wept openly then. "Think of what you're giving up! You can't get married, have children. You'll never be able to make a baby with her. Your love can *never* make a baby!"

It's true I always imagined I would have children, that when September came, I would walk with my sons and daughters down a lane covered with auburn leaves and wait on a quiet corner until their school bus came. Of course it's still possible, as anything is, but I am no longer counting on the future to redeem the present. I prefer to view my life the other way around.

*If this be error and upon me proved,*
*I never writ, nor no man ever loved.*

## Daffodils

*(Narcissus species) Upright, slender, medium green leaves. Flower consists of a flattened round base (perianth) with wavy margin and a cup-shaped center (corona), often in a contrasting color.*

Confession:

When I brought you the flowers, they were also for me. Perhaps they were the gift I secretly desired. Because it is hard to resist giving others what we want for ourselves. Because I love you, and daffodils too.

But that day, caught in a rainstorm, I ducked into a flower shop on Forbes Avenue. Of the wide array of roses and tulips, carnations and lilies, they were these flowers—orange at the center and green at the stems—that beckoned to me from their dark woven basket.

"I'll take a bunch of daffodils," I said, and the woman wrapped them in tissue, then cellophane, and pushed a small square of paper toward me.

"For the card," she said—in case I was unfamiliar with the ritual.

I hesitated, because I knew this bouquet might mean nothing to you. But they were beautiful, and it felt wrong to keep them all to myself, so I brought them to your office and laid them on your desk, and the card, bubbled from rain with blue ink bleeding, said only:

"The perfect contrast..." which was plainspoken, the way you prefer; which was impressive, coming from me.

**Corsage Orchid**
*(Cattleya labiata) C. labiata is one of the most vigorous Cattleya species and undoubtedly the easiest to grow. After flowering, it should be allowed to rest, and water should be given sparingly. Too much water during its rest period will rot the roots and hinder growth in the spring. These orchids generate huge, frilled flowers in pinks, purples, yellows, and whites, reminiscent of prom dresses and other formal gowns.*

At the Christmas party, when the men and women danced together, each accepted and acknowledged couple in his suit and her flowing gown, I must admit I admired them: their fearless interaction with the other's form, their practiced symmetry of motion. They did not see it as an act of "entitlement." They did not imagine anyone had been "excluded." But suddenly, all I could think of was taking your hand and walking out onto that island of light.

*Dance with me, I want my arm about you, the charm about you, will carry me through to ...*

Two men from our table excused themselves. They had put in their appearance but wearied quickly of the pretense. Everywhere the couples like tops of wedding cakes, and our sore-thumbishness: the pieces of a set that didn't match.

*... Heaven, I'm in Heaven, and my heart beats so that I can hardly speak, and I seem to find the happiness I seek ...*

At home in stocking feet with Joni Mitchell serenading, we discover a dance without spectacle that leads where the music does not follow.

**Forget • Me • Nots**

*(Myosotidium Hortensia) Legend has it that in medieval times, a knight and his lady were walking along the side of a river. He picked a posy of flowers, but because of the weight of his armor, he fell into the river. As he was drowning, he threw the posy to his loved one and shouted, "Forget-me-not!" This is a flower connected with romance and tragic fate. It was often worn by ladies as a sign of faithfulness and enduring love.*

I begin to forget my life before you, and then to forget I have forgotten. The past swells with imaginative amnesia, and I begin to remember you in places you could not have been!

*Do you see us? Smoking cigarettes on the back steps of the Catholic school after the nuns had all gone home. Flicking our ashes in unison.*

Then the future also, in luminous palimpsest: what I see is our lives branching together, the letters of our stories intertwined; tracing your script like ivy, like the dotted lines in a cursive book for a sentence that is not yet finished.

**Sword Lily**

*(Gladiolus) Funnel-shaped florets arranged tightly along a stout spike with blooms opening from bottom to top. Possesses a strong, geotropic response and will bend toward the light. Parts of the plant body are poisonous to the touch and tongue.*

"Love, as you know, is a harrowing event"—Anne Carson wrote, and she was right.

It is difficult at times to determine what you are fighting for and what you are fighting against. I remember the day you told me, "I don't want to spend my life defending my life; I want to spend my life living it."

I agreed, my whole body sighing its consensus. Yet how does this living happen? How do we surrender our weapons without forfeiting the war?

Sometimes when I am indicted for aberrant deeds, when the eyes at the copy machine avert suddenly or focus a little too hard—as if determined to see through me—I remember that I do not walk the same in the world as I did before, my arm slung easily through a man's. I muse again: there is something wrong with a world where women's value is contingent upon their escorts.

*What is the worst name anyone has ever called you?* Lesbian. (I meant it, too.)

Because for a name to be real, it must be chosen. For a label to stick, it must hold true in some heartfelt and unassailable way.

Remember when we first left the comforts of the West Coast for the startling topography of the future? Time and space, both moving forward and out of our hands, gritty under the car wheels and the fingernails. It was all anticipation, which is terror and joy blurring the lines like a car winding down a steep road at dusk.

I don't think I had ever felt judged before—not so palpably that my skin turned splotchy and goose-bumped and my throat became hoarse—until we stopped to eat in a quaint restaurant, just south of Cannon Beach off Highway 101 in Oregon. The Pig 'n' Pancake it was called. There was one in Seaside too, and a little further north, in Astoria. My parents used to bring me there on family vacations, one of the few times we ate out all year. I loved the pink booths and paper napkins (the ones at home were cloth), and sitting up to the table and choosing a meal meant partaking of any possibility. *So many choices.*

But that day in Cannon Beach, the dark stares of strangers with their children, reading us over their spectacles, studying us as if to calculate the precise nature and ratio of threat. I felt monstrous, looming, as if everyone were cowering at my feet, then rising up, slowly, to meet me at my height. All I had wanted was breakfast, but I sensed from every solemn face that we weren't wanted there. Not our short hair, not our out-of-state plates, not our un-ringed fingers and the confidence that carried us, first to our table, and shortly thereafter, away.

It is a different world since loving you, I can't pretend. People don't smile at me the way they used to: that friendly human generosity, expecting nothing in return. Sometimes I miss it. Maybe that's cowardly of me. Maybe that's weak. But in my own love, always, I grow stronger.

**Wallflower**

(Cheiranthus) Old-fashioned, profuse, bright-orange garden flower that tends to "bloom itself to death." Short flowering season, unreliably perennial, and an infamous lure for butterflies.

I am no good at parties, especially arriving alone. I stand too long in the doorway, as if trying to decide, *can I still escape? will anyone notice me slipping away?*

That night in October, my first excursion of graduate school, I deliberated about my bottle of wine: share with a room full of strangers, or go home and drink it alone?

You were there, the girl from class with the vibrant eyes, blue like a raspberry ICEE. (And why are those blue to begin with?)

You were drinking blackberry wheat beer, your hair pulled back from your face. I approached you at once, and we commenced a conversation without struggle. None of the awkwardness, none of the familiar foreboding. *Yes,* I thought, *I'd like to learn more about her. Listen to the way her words come soft and sharp like arrows from a supple bow.*

I left early that night, suddenly nervous, despite your best-intentioned offer to take me home. What was it I was so afraid of? The ease or the intensity? The possibility of what reactions our chemistry might ignite?

To this day, I am not sure we have ever finished that conversation. I watch for the little blue ellipses that connect our thoughts and fractured sentences.

*We shall not cease from exploration,*
*and the end of all our exploring*
*will be to arrive where we started from*
*and know the place for the first time.*
—T.S. Eliot, from *The Four Quartets*

I want the circuitous conversation, prolepsis, catharsis. I want the gentle waver of the tongue, and each story upon another time.

## Pink Lady's Slipper

*(Cypripedium acaule) Endangered wildflower, which takes a long time to grow and is often collected by orchid lovers. The plant has only two leaves, which are green and branch out from the stem like a child's drawing. The deep pink flower, which resembles a ballet shoe, is unique in that it remains tightly closed except for a small opening. It generally grows in shady forests under pines, oaks, red maples, and sweetgum trees.*

In the old days, I used to sell shoes, and after hours attending to feet I did not know, I became convinced the foot was the ugliest part of the body. Those nubby toes! Those calloused heels! Who could love a thing so vile?

Then, I met you, and even your toes were interesting, even your heels worthy of pumice-love and wild profusions of kisses.

With you, I never seem to have my feet on the ground. Always a trailing of cloud lace, some whimsy swaddled around.

You have seen me on my right foot, my wrong foot, always struggling to put the best one forward.

You have felt my cold feet quiver, casting back the dangling fiancé.

*My sprung feet, my stunned feet, my feet of clay.*

And in all these things, I am at your feet, on your side, under your wing, bright in the eyes with longing.

Until I have one foot in the grave, and then the other, I will love you as I have never loved another.

## Iris

*These flowers have three petals called the "standards," and three outer petal-like sepals called the "falls." Once flower buds reach maturity, the base of the flower elongates to push the bud out from the sheath that surrounds it. Once extended, flower opening occurs.*

*You're just too good to be true. Can't take my eyes off of you . . .*

"Always with the old songs," you say. "Always with the premature retrospectives."

But what's the crime in looking back as we move forward? In the picture swelling to panorama the way a barren garden suddenly springs to bloom?

Iris: the goddess of the rainbow and messenger of the gods.

Iris: The pigmented, round, contractile membrane of the eye, suspended between the cornea and lens and perforated by the pupil. It regulates the amount of light entering the eye.

Iris: Any of numerous plants of the genus *Iris*, having narrow, sword-shaped leaves and showy, variously colored flowers.

Iris: A rainbow or rainbow-like display of colors.

So many colors in potential . . . So many possible meanings . . .

*You're just too good to be true. I can't take my eyes off of you.*

## Rose

*(Rosa) Intricate flower characterized by strong fragrance in many varieties, soft petals, and stems lined with thorns. The most popular flower of the romance industry, the rose now blossoms naturally in every color but blue.*

We want the impossible: immortality, easy love, sufficient passion, reckless freedom, and abundant cushions when we fall. We are wise to remember what the Spanish say: *No hay rosas sin espinas.* There are no roses without thorns.

And while I know full well roses are not the answer—or even the first curled frond of the explanation— it feels good, again, to be told we are beautiful, to blush once more in a lover's arms.

*Once again, desire—*
*That looser of limbs and bitterly sweet—*
*Makes me to tremble.*
*You are irresistible . . .*
—Sappho, Fragment 130

If I could, I would give you a blue rose—its sumptuous paradox, its bittersweet beauty.

V

# Carapace

For a long time, everything only happened to other people. Dreams were for sleep, and hunger was for waking; breakfast for morning and supper for evening—a whole world plotted at coordinate points, the axis of which was witness.

Families looked alike and answered to the same names. School was a turnstile of listening and lurching suddenly forward. Churchgoers faithfully covered their heads. (Why did they do this? Was God offended by hair?) And the sprinklers came on before the sun came up, and the flag came down before the sun disappeared, and there were whole locked chambers in the middle of the day, while children were napping, when secret business was silently conducted.

What I knew of the world I learned from simple observations and from stories. Stories belonged to books, which were their literal dwelling places, and books became the rough and ragged cottages that characters called home. Like me, they dreamed and hungered, considered obedience and conformity, gazed curiously across the sinews of the world, in which they were not yet, or fully, enfolded.

We were the watchers then, of vicarious vocation—standing on the life-docks, untying the knots—notaries of the Goodship's passage.

≈

The first funeral I ever attended was Humpty Dumpty's. His death occurred without warning, or precedent, as I sifted the pages of my Mother Goose book:

> *Humpty Dumpty sat on a wall*
> *Humpty Dumpty had a great fall*
> *And all the king's horses and all the king's men*
> *Couldn't put Humpty together again*

The rhyme, arresting in its sadness, compelling first by its seeming randomness—*Was it foul play? The shoddy laying of stones? How had Humpty come to fall at all?*—and then by its plaintive hopelessness. Could there be no reassemblage? Did no one own a glue gun? Was this truly the end of him, shell of his former self, muted and concrete-cracked?

Lexicon-building: *Euphemism*, from the Greek for "good speech"; the way no one would say he was *dead*, only that he had *fallen*.

≈

In Vacation Bible School, we read a story called "The Fall of Man." I imagine mountains, one helpless body hurtling over a cliff, plunging toward the craggy ravine below. In *my* story, he pulls the rip cord attached to his knapsack and, all at once, an explosion of color: the parachute swirls red and gold, enlarging to fill the cloud-crowded horizon. And the man is safe and happy. And the world does not end.

"Open your Bibles to Genesis, Chapter 3," our teacher instructs. As she moves through the words on the onion-skinned page, I follow them each with my finger. The title says nothing of women, nothing of snakes, and there is no tumbling, no crumbling, no collapse. What's more: I'm not fond of this character called the "LORD God." Why did he plant the fruit tree there in the first place if he didn't want his garden party to eat?

Now the teacher leans a felt board on her easel. She places a man-figure called Adam (though he resembles Barbie's Ken) beside a tall green tree brimming with apples. Beside Adam, she adds a woman-figure called Eve, and beside her, a long, uncoiled serpent who she reminds us is Satan in disguise. "Why are Adam and Eve banished from the Garden? What did they do wrong?"

A dozen hands jut eagerly into the air. The general consensus: "Because they disobeyed God!"

"And what is it called when people disobey God?" Her eyes narrow on mine, and I look down at my book as a flush floods my face. "Julie?"

After some hesitation, I repeat my own crime, what my mother says I am increasingly guilty of: "Acting out?"

"*Sin*," she clarifies. "God tested Adam, and Adam failed the test. He got a big F on his report card next to Obedience, and as a result, he had to be punished." Between the tree and the two humans, Mrs. Walters inserts an angry-looking angel waving a fire-rimmed sword.

"All of you memorized a Bible verse yesterday about sin. Do you remember? It begins: 'And the wages of sin . . . ' How does it end?"

Another flock of fluttering hands, and someone shouts an answer: "The wages of sin is *death*."

Now Death I understand. Death is Humpty Dumpty split open on the sidewalk and "lights out" and going to sleep and never waking up—a night with no morning to follow. Mrs. Walters reminds us "the gift of God is eternal life through Jesus Christ," but because he was hungry, Adam has been condemned to die, and Eve was only trying to be helpful, and Jesus doesn't exist yet if you read the book in order, and I am still not sure what any of this has to do with falling. The teacher says we are all already fallen, even if we have no scrapes to show for it, no bloody knees or broken limbs. The sin original, the fate inevitable: inside each of us thumps a fierce and fractured heart.

Lexicon-building: *Felix culpa*, from the Latin for "fortunate fall"; wherein a series of miserable events leads to an ultimately happier outcome. Enter Icarus. Enter Sisyphus. Enter my mother, who says I am "headed for a fall."

≈

If there were Chosen People in the childhood world, then Sarah Hodson must have been one of them. Small for her age, with a nymph's demure voice and dancing eyes and tiny diamonds garnishing her ears, she reeked of sweetness, sliding easily into any unoccupied lap, earning the praise of all who observed her.

An ordinary day. We sat in our chairs around the oblong, crayon-marred table. Mrs. Whitehair instructed us to "stay inside the lines." We learned the names of the first three presidents, whose silhouettes were construction-papered on the wall. For snack: frozen cups of half peach sherbet, half vanilla ice cream, consumed with a tiny, wooden spoon.

Sarah Hodson was absent. Mrs. Whitehair conferred with the principal in the doorway. Suddenly, we were all instructed to stand and hold hands and pray: "God bless Sarah Hodson, and be with her today. God bless Sarah Hodson, and be with her today." I wanted to know why Sarah Hodson in particular, and why today in particular, but Mrs. Whitehair held a long finger over her lips and frowned.

That night at the dinner table, I asked my parents why the sadness at school, and the phone tree, and the preparation of casseroles.

"Is this little girl a friend of yours?" my father asked.

"No."

To my mother: "Well, that's a relief." She passed him a plate of steaming spinach.

"What happened to her? Why wasn't she at school?"

"There was an accident," my mother said.

"What kind of accident?"

"Eat your meat."

"I don't like it."

"I'm sure everything will be fine," my father murmured. "Don't worry your pretty little head—"

"Is Sarah Hodson going to die?"

A long silence before my mother put down her knife and replied: "It's possible. She's in a very deep sleep, and no one knows if she's going to wake up."

Lexicon-building: *Coma*, from the Greek for "deep sleep"; often occurs following trauma to the skull. Think of Sleeping Beauty. Think of Rip Van Winkle. Think of spells, which also must be broken.

"I want to know what happened," I say to my father. He sits on the edge of my bed, pulls the covers close to my chin, a phenomenon he calls *tucking*.

"I know you do, honey, but I don't want it to upset you. I don't want you to have any more bad dreams."

"Do you think Sarah is dreaming right now? And is she in her own bed or a hospital bed?"

He sighs. "When Sarah was walking to school this morning, she didn't cross in the crosswalk like she was supposed to. She probably didn't even look both ways. She saw somebody she knew, and she ran out in the street, and she got hit by a car."

"But she lives on the same street as our school."

"I know."

"And we have a crossing guard."

"I know."

"Did the car run her over, or did she just bounce off the hood?"

"I don't think we should talk about that," he replies. "She's in the hospital now, and her family is there, and the doctors are doing everything they can. She's broken some bones and cracked a rib, but with the right care and plenty of prayers, she can heal."

"Will she have to wear a mummy suit?"

"I don't know."

"Will she have amnesia when she wakes up?"

"I don't think so."

"Will she still be as pretty as she was before?"

He kisses my forehead. That's how I know I've gone too far. "Goodnight, young lady. Sleep tight."

But I can't sleep, and as soon as my father is gone, I sit up in bed and switch on the light. The following are problems with this story:

• *Absent antagonist.* Who is responsible for Sarah's injuries? Did God smote her; is being hit by a car evidence of smoting? Most believers would say God allowed it to happen. Maybe God was testing her, lured by a friend peddling fresh peaches or clusters of caution-yellow bananas. So if Sarah failed the test, maybe *she* is to blame: running out into traffic, not even looking both ways. . . . Can you be the victim and the villain of your own story? But what about the negligent crossing guard or the driver of the anonymous car or the witnesses, puttying our narrative gaps, suturing our questions along a seam of closure?

• *Lack of motive.* To the best of anyone's knowledge, this is a motiveless crime, which makes it a non-crime, which leaves us with that empty bowl of a word called *accident.* Scrape the porcelain as many times as you like, but no porridge there, no sustenance. And because Sarah was more beloved than most people, because her beauty and innocence were so widely and effusively lauded, what shield might any of us have hoped for? If what we deserve is not what we receive, and vice versa, then the world is a wild machine, plowing these fields at random.

• *Lack of moral.* I have learned nothing new from this story. Being careful, looking both ways . . . I had been told already, as Sarah had, but the knowledge did not save her, and likewise, would not protect me from harm. The unexpected was too powerful, unstaking claims to mastery, reinventing the familiar as foreign. She walked that way every day. She did as she was told. Her mother watched from the upstairs window of their house with the slanted roof, a baby on her bony hip and the curtain drawn back like a veil.

≈

In October, every year, we marked the end of Daylight Savings, the pleasure of falling back, with a ritual we called *the hollowing*. It began with a venture to the pumpkin patch and culminated with the lighting of a jack-o-lantern, which seemed an allegory for the strange ways in which all of us are capable of being transformed.

To carve a pumpkin is to enter its body with an intimacy I perceived intensely but could not find words for. My father steadied my hand as I drove the blade through the pumpkin's thick skin, dragging it counterclockwise to create a lid. My mother covered the kitchen table with newspapers; my father and I donned our matching floral aprons. He turned the pumpkin over on its side and began to cut away the orange cords of flesh, tethering stem to base. I could not have known then how sexual it was, easing my hand into the exhilarating darkness of pith and seed, touching the slope of the firm walls and the soft, unusual interior. I felt reverent toward my task and approached it with uncustomary quietness and concentration: scooping out the tendrils, rinsing the seeds in a colander for my mother to roast, olive oil snapping in her scalding pan.

As we collaborated to create the pumpkin's face, the ridged canvas awkwardly transfigured in our human likeness, I imagined the dramatic determinations of God. Was this how we also had been devised—haphazardly, with a scalpel in one hand and a Sharpie in the other? Were we God's whims, his seasonal decorations, pleasing shells he lit with candles for a spell, then watched as we grew gray, blew out, sunk in at the center, gave over (inevitably) to rot and decay? There was nothing sadder, I thought, than the sight of a pumpkin shriveling on someone's back porch, surrounded by bags of compost, soggy from the bleak November rain. For this reason perhaps, I often turned pensive after our work was done, regarding the jack-o-lantern with a romantic regret (that we had defiled it) and also with a vague disappointment (that it did not resemble the Platonic Pumpkin of the mind's perfectionist eye).

Lexicon-building: *Deism*, from the Latin for "god"; belief in a deity who created the world but has since remained indifferent to it; see also *clockwork universe*, wherein said deity winds the clock of the world along gears governed by laws of science. No parting of the Red Sea. No miracle with loaves and fishes. Theology in place of religion. Parables without supernatural powers.

On Halloween night, it was our custom to read "The Legend of Sleepy Hollow." I had seen the Disney animated version also, which superimposed itself over the rich, archaic language of Irving's nerve-tingling tale:

"'Certain it is,'" my father commenced, his voice deliberately low and slow, with his arm wrapped comfortingly around my shoulder, "'the place still continues under the sway of some witching power, that holds a spell over the minds of the good people, causing them to walk in a continual reverie. They are given to all kinds of marvellous beliefs, are subject to trances and visions, and frequently see strange sights, and hear music and voices in the air. . . .'"

I would begin to shiver from the mere ambiance of Sleepy Hollow, pulling candy corns from the pockets of my pajamas and stuffing them anxiously into my mouth at each (albeit predictable) twist of the plot. How to explain: it was both fear I craved and fear I longed to curtail, as in facing the fear, as in confronting at last the headless figure lurking in alleyways and under rain-soaked awnings in my own troubling, marathon dreams. How to explain: the story never became tiresome or tame, despite hearing it year after year, despite discussing with my father how Brom Bones was the most likely culprit, how Ichabod's own fears get the better of him, drive him into embarrassed exile.

"Look here," my father would say, pointing to the phenomenon called *foreshadowing*—a word neither of us had learned but that would become increasingly relevant over the span of our years: "' . . . Brom Van Brunt, the hero of the country round, which rang with his feats of strength and hardihood. From his Herculean frame and great powers of limb he had received the nick name of Brom Bones, by which he was universally known. He was famed for great knowledge and skill in horsemanship, being as dexterous on horseback as a Tartar.' And later, what do we learn? 'Brom Bones, too, who, shortly after his rival's disappearance conducted the blooming Katrina in triumph to the altar, was observed to look exceedingly knowing whenever the story of Ichabod was related, and always burst into a hearty laugh at the mention of the pumpkin;

which led some to suspect that he knew more about the matter than he chose to tell.'"

Still, I favored an alternative explanation: that Ichabod Crane had been the victim of a ghostly crime for which Brom Bones preferred to take credit. He let rumors of his mischief churn rather than admit they were not alone in those woods, not safe from the stalking supervision of a "galloping Hessman," who rode every night, blind and crazed, in search of the body to yield his future head.

When I was scared and dove beneath the blankets, my father would suggest a different story. At once, my head resurfaced on the pillow, and I begged him not to stop reading again. Because as much as I longed to follow Ichabod to his moment of doom—his desperate ride to the bridge—I also longed for a taste of his courtship, however ill-fated, with the "country coquette" called Katrina Van Tassel. In the movie, she wore a peach dress puffed out at the waist and cascading down to the floor in a graceful, old-fashioned way. She carried a parasol, that emblem of elegance and femininity, what Marta had wanted for her seventh birthday in *The Sound of Music*. I too asked for a parasol and received one, but the feeling was less spectacular, twirling it under my own hand, raising it over my own head, than watching Katrina do so and looking on with Ichabod and Brom in a state of prickling hypnosis, an aching hunger so deep in my gut I thought it a bellyache from too much Halloween candy.

Lexicon-building: *Foreshadowing,* a literary term associated with "prolepsis" or "prefiguration"; suggesting the placement of important clues to prepare the reader for twists of plot to follow.

≈

Mrs. Olsen, the school librarian, announces that this month we are going to read autobiographies. "Can anyone tell me what this means?" And I can because I have read autobiographies before!

"They're stories written by people about their own experiences—but different from diaries, because they're meant for other people to see."

"Good." She smiles at me, and I bask in the warm glow of adult approval. "Now can anyone tell me the difference between an *auto*biography and a *bio*graphy?"

I sit up tall on my knees; my hand jettisons above my classmates' heads. "Anyone else?" She scans the room, searching for another volunteer. Conceding at last: "Julie?"

"Autobiography means when the person telling the story is the person who actually *lived* the story. Biography means a writer is reporting on the life of someone else. Biographies can be authorized or unauthorized."

As I look around the room, pleased by the high bookshelves nearly occluding the windows and the commingling odors of dusty hardbacks like *The Count of Monte Cristo* and clean, crisp pages of *The Babysitter's Club* and *Sweet Valley High*, I notice also the contemptuous faces of my classmates, arranged on the rug in cadres of their own choosing, the gulf around me ever-widening.

When it is time to select our autobiographies, I proceed at once to the appropriate section of the Dewey Decimal System, only to find I recognize every spine. "Mrs. Olsen, I've already read all these books." Erica Gregory says something mocking behind me, accompanied by a chorus of squawking laughter.

"That's impossible, dear. We have over a hundred of them." She lifts her glasses from the chain around her neck and begins reading off a series of titles, my own voice interjecting—"Yes, I've read it." . . . "That one too." . . . "Oh, that was a really good one."

After some negotiation, it is decided that I will go with my mother after school to the Southwest Public Library, where I have gotten in trouble before for speaking too loud and for squealing with delight and for not understanding that a library is "a sanctuary, not a live bidding auction," and there I will choose an autobiography from this much greater selection. We go, and I am overwhelmed (as always) by the Jenga maze of books, the puzzling and provocative sea of choices, so my mother, in her increasing exasperation, selects an autobiography for me:

"I read this book in the '70s," she says, "but the message is still relevant today." I place my red plastic Q card on the counter, barcode up, and study the laminated photograph on the cover: *Joni: An Unforgettable Story*.

Lexicon-building: *Sanctuary*, from Middle English, Old French, and Late Latin for "a sacred place" or "private room." The word promises protection, as in the most holy region of a church nearest the altar; as in refuge or immunity granted to fugitives; as in a nature preserve where birds and wildlife, especially those hunted for sport, can thrive and breed safely.

The water is my sanctuary. It has been so since the first time my father lifted me onto his sunburned shoulders and plunged me into the roiling waves. From our house on a hill overlooking the sea, we walk down to the rocky lip of Puget Sound and wander a great distance—two or three miles—from the Fauntleroy ferry docks to the looming bulkheads of Loman Park, where the NO TRESPASSING signs of private residences sprout like blades of recalcitrant grass. Where large, kelp-belted logs have washed up on shore, we climb them. Pretending all else around us has turned (quicksand-quick) to swamp, we build our bridge, one log to the next, charting a course from these natural high-rises to the barnacled stairs that carried us away from danger. We often sit on the ledge for hours, feet dangling, salty wind rifling our hair; we lay out our shells like hallowed currency, placing small pebble bets and skipping smooth, polished stones across the water.

"I learned a new riddle," I tell my father. "Wanna hear it?"

"Sure."

"What does a fish say when he hits his head on a wall?"

His hands crinkle inside windbreaker pockets. "I don't know...I give up."

"Dam!" And before he can respond, I quickly explain: "It's not a swear word, though. It's spelled the other way—d-a-m, like a beaver dam."

"That's a good one," my father says. "Now I have a riddle for you. What do you a call a turtle without a shell? Is he naked or homeless?"

Puzzled, I sit quietly for a while, arranging my bronze agates and hinged clamshells in a hierarchy of imagined worth. "Isn't a turtle a turtle *because* of his shell? I don't see how he could exist without one."

"But what if he did? Would he be naked or homeless?"

This question perplexes me as much as the one in theology—*can God build a rock so big he cannot move it?* And when Carl Lull asked the question (to be difficult, of course), the teacher was thoughtful and deliberate in her reply: "God calls upon us to have faith and not to test him. God does not participate in contests." (Which was a shame, I thought, and a waste of omnipotence. Think about the gunny-sack races and the making of paper cranes. How everyone would want God on her team . . . )

"This isn't a funny riddle, Dad. Does it even have a punch line?"

He pats my head and eases his long body down to the sand, stands facing me framed by sailboats sporting their sundry shields and driftwood enshrining his shoes: "Punch lines are for jokes," my father says. "Riddles aren't meant to be easy."

That night in my little boat of a bed, I opened Joni Eareckson's story. Her face on the cover appeared eerily familiar, beach-tanned and bright-eyed, accessible and reassuring as the sister I never had. But why, I wondered, was she clenching a pen in her teeth, and what was this small but sprawling word printed below the copyright next to "personal narrative"? I sounded it out: *tet-ra-ple-gi-a.* Maybe a dinosaur, I thought—or a skin condition.

"The hot July sun was setting low in the west and gave the waters of Chesapeake Bay a warm red glow. The water was murky, and as my body broke the surface in a dive, its cold cleanness doused my skin." I knew that feeling: the inexplicable comfort of the first chill, the deftly orchestrated pleasure of the plunge. " . . . Panic seized me. With all my willpower and strength, I tried to break free. Nothing happened . . . I felt the pressure of holding my breath begin to build . . . Another tidal swell gently lifted me. Fragments of faces, thoughts, and memories spun crazily across my consciousness. My friends. My parents. Things I was ashamed of. Maybe God was calling me to come and explain these actions."

I bit my lip, a habit my mother was trying to break me of. Each time the flesh blistered over, I tore it open again with my teeth, often absently, without thinking. Each time I was frightened or pensive, I took refuge in that brief, acute, but tolerable—and this was the crucial part—pain. I controlled what happened to me, even as I had no say whatsoever in what happened to other people. "The next tidal swell was a little stronger than the rest and lifted me a bit higher. I fell back on the bottom, with broken shells, stones, and sand grating into my shoulders and face. . . . "

Then, the moment of foreshadowing, which I had come to recognize and even expect: more subtle than angels bearing bold annunciations, but a similarly prophetic ideal: "At last, somewhere on my body, I could feel something. As I lay there on the sand, I began to piece things together. I had hit my head diving; I must have injured something to cause this numbness. I wondered how long it would last. 'Don't worry,' I reassured Butch and Kathy—and myself. 'The Lord won't let anything happen to me. I'll be all right.'"

But something had *already* happened! I understood implicitly and with a growing horror. Joni wasn't going to walk again or dive into the sea at sunset or ever regain feeling in the lower part of her body. She would be a talking head, dead below the shoulders, like a mannequin whose limbs could be arranged, contorted, even removed without her knowledge or consent. The idea of it—to lose those tactile powers to which I was most deeply attached—seemed in fact a "fate worse than death," which was a phrase I had heard volleyed overhead by grown-ups who could not have possibly understood its gravity the way I did then. I was angry with my mother for making me read this story, for claiming it conveyed a timeless message. What could that message be? That the universe was only hapless currents crossing in apathy? That no one was safe and nothing could be explained? Distressed by these prospects, I struggled to conceive an alternative.

Each week in school, we copied down a long series of words from the chalkboard, the spellings of which we would memorize and the meanings of which we would learn. Part of learning a meaning meant using the dictionary to locate a word's origin, pronunciation, and definition, followed by a careful cross-check in the thesaurus for its synonyms and antonyms. *Arbitrary* had been recently assigned, and in my notes, I wrote the following: denotation— "based on or subject to individual discretion or preference or sometimes impulse or whim"; <u>synonyms</u>—*uncertain, random, accidental, discretionary*; <u>antonyms</u>—*calculated, reasonable, rational, scientific.* I found this word elegant and enigmatic, its four syllables bobbing like a buoy over the smooth waves of sound. But just as Mrs. Miller had predicted, this hypothetical word suddenly *applied* to something—a concept, and a means for that concept's articulation.

Life either must be arbitrary, or it must not. I wavered on the binary bridge a moment, steadied myself. This was no solid bridge but one strung together with wooden planks and fraying ropes: a consciousness given to sway. If nothing is random, then mustn't everything be planned? Did God really have the option of indifference, or was he in fact the sole and master arbiter of suffering—disguised as punishment—plucking off pieces from the human checkerboard?

I began to read again in pursuit of clarification. In science class, we learned that all hypotheses must be tested for their validity. What had Joni done to *deserve* her fate? Was she culpable in some way that could be proven? My mother insisted that Pollyanna's fall from the tall tree outside her bedroom window was a direct result of disobedience. The nature of her injuries was not discussed with the same meticulous detail as Joni's, perhaps because Pollyanna herself was not telling the story (biography, not autobiography). However, neither Pollyanna nor Joni Eareckson was able to walk again as a consequence of her particular experience. Joni did not appear to have been breaking the rules when she dove into Chesapeake Bay, yet she recounted in the time prior to her injury, that sometimes she'd "even climb down the drain pipe outside [her] bedroom window and meet [her boyfriend] after curfew." Eventually, her mother caught her sneaking out, and from then on, her adherence to household rules was more strictly enforced.

But she didn't fall then, not literally. The old connection between falling and sin resurfaced as I read Joni's accounts of her romance with Jason and her difficulty "dealing with the problems of temptation." She seemed at this point in her story to be writing in code—nothing concrete or explicit, only euphemistic statements like "Before we realized what was happening, innocent, youthful expressions of love for one another—hand-holding, hugging, kissing—gave way to caressing, touching, and passions neither of us could control." Did this mean "sex"? Was she referring to the "slippery slope" my mother had warned me about? Was she also referring back to her thoughts while drowning of "things she was ashamed of"? And the most important question of all—did Joni lose feeling in her lower body *because* she had used this body for sexual pleasure outside of marriage in the way that God expressly forbids?

Certainly I saw a correlation, but there was no firm evidence of causality, which was—as I had been told—the real work of science: proving things. As I read on, my feelings for Joni grew stronger—not in the "Katrina way," as I had come to regard it whenever a woman aroused in me some more riveted attention accompanied by physical reaction (the tensing of calves, the sweating of palms . . . )—but a kind of empathy began to emerge, as though *her* story might have been *my* story; as if we were, in a way, the same person. What frightened me most was not, ultimately, this newfound fear of diving and the water or how I too might lose the use of my body, despite every possible precaution taken, despite resolute observance of curfews that I didn't yet have and the oppressive sense of my own interminable purity. (It seemed unthinkable that anyone would ever want me the way Jason had wanted Joni. . . . ) Rather, I was frightened by Joni's reconciliation with God, her growing insistence that nothing was arbitrary, that all was predestined—God had made a plan for her life, and through faith, she would graciously accept it.

Lexicon-building: *Paralysis*, from the Greek meaning "to loosen or disable on one side." As in a literal impairment of voluntary motion. As in any state of complete stoppage or perceived helplessness.

≈

My father's turtle riddle returns to haunt me. What is a turtle without a shell? What is a human without a body—or with a damaged body, distorted, immobilized, or incomplete? The two questions seem analogous on purpose, and both concern the problem of the stuff inside. There is that longing to enter things and to be enveloped by them: the warm house on the rainy night, the sensual interior of the pumpkin, even the small bathroom stall on an airplane and the satisfied click of the OCCUPIED slate in the door. There is also that longing to be inside other bodies, which—as a girl, a future woman and intended wife and mother; as a "vessel," to use the poetic term—I have learned implicitly is an aberrant desire.

On my own time, I have been studying the intricate vocabulary of fear. I am particularly interested in *phobias*, which are long-lasting fears distinguished by their acuteness and irrationality. Claustrophobia is a common one, meaning "fear of closed spaces." Perhaps birds hatch because they grow claustrophobic inside the egg. Perhaps corn is relieved when freed from its husk and peas when liberated from their pods. But I seem to suffer from the antonym—*agoraphobia*—meaning "fear of open spaces," which is what most of the world seems to offer. I perceive the tremendous vulnerability of crossing through traffic, how pedestrians appear daily "to take their lives in their hands." On the chairlift at the Fiorini ski school, I kept to my seat, even when the moment came to dismount. I couldn't proceed onto the daunting openness of the mountain, its incessantly white invitation; so I went round again like a rider on a carousel, the teacher distressed and waving his hands and all the other children laughing.

There was no right answer to the riddle, but how you answered said something about how you saw the world. If the turtle is *naked* without his shell, then the shell itself must be equivalent to clothing: an accessory "added on" to the real being, something ornamental and disposable, not part of the essence or core. But if the turtle is *homeless*, then the separation between Physical/Tangible and Whatever Else There Is decreases from a cavern to a sliver, the schism between "body" and "soul" shrinks significantly, is perhaps eliminated all together. Once again, the pressure building up in me—reminiscent of pickle jars, the black rubber grip from the silverware drawer, and the strain of breaking that seal. How necessary it seemed to choose between extremes: faith or doubt, destiny or puppetry, the Almighty God or the Big Bang Theory. Paralyzed, I retreat further inward. I look for books that promise nothing but easy answers. I use a kickboard in the swimming pool and keep my head resolutely above water.

Lexicon-building: *Agnosticism*, from the Greek for "not known"; an intellectual doctrine or attitude affirming the uncertainty of all claims to ultimate knowledge. Think of "the rock and the hard place." Think of the "double-edged sword."

≈

Then the day arrived when the students in my middle school (who were also the students in my Confirmation class) traveled several hours away to spend a weekend at the Lutheran Bible Institute. It was explained to us by our teacher and pastor that "spiritual rejuvenation" was expected to take place, once we were removed from the noises and hazards of the city. It had also been explained to me personally that outside the constraints of the classroom, I was expected to "come out of my shell."

Since my first fairy tales, I had been uneasy about the forest. Riding Hood had gotten into trouble with the Wolf, Hansel and Gretel with the Witch, and Goldilocks (though notably her fault) with the Three (less than gregarious) Bears. And then there was Ichabod on his decrepit steed, desperate for a clearing in the midst of the effusive, overshadowing trees: "The night grew darker and darker; the stars seemed to sink deeper in the sky, and driving clouds occasionally hid them from his sight. He had never felt so lonely and dismal."

Lonely and dismal also, confined to a tiny dormitory in the middle of the woods, I leaned out the window in search of stars. Since my life had been parsed into two alternative pastimes—reading and brooding—the pressure to socialize, to be friendly with my peers, proved all the more demoralizing, and I receded from it like a waning moon. Unzipping my backpack, I withdrew a new book, a *children's* book—which typically I passed over with disdain—but this one fastened itself to my attention with a provocative, two-word title: *Tuck Everlasting.* "Tuck," which I associated with a mandate to sleep, was here paired with "Everlasting," suggesting immortality or an unchanging state. I wondered if this would be a story of someone in a coma.

Settling down on the thin mattress with the rough orange blanket, I began to read in silence: "There was something strange about the wood. If the look of the first house suggested that you'd better pass it by, so did the look of the wood, but for quite a different reason. The house was so proud of itself that you wanted to make a lot of noise as you passed, and maybe even throw a rock or two. But the wood had a sleeping, otherworld appearance that made you want to speak in whispers . . . "

At the mirror, Kendra Kostrich, my random-assignment roommate for the trip, fussed with her hair, raised it up in a ponytail, tightened the hair band, then let it fall back down again. Finally, she sighed loudly and whirled around.

"I'm bored! When are the activities supposed to start?"

I looked up, shrugged my shoulders, and continued reading. I had become engrossed by the introduction of a character named Winnie Foster, a girl just slightly younger than I and with a similar problem. As she explained: "'If I had a sister or a brother, there'd be someone else for them to watch. But, as it is, there's only me. I'm tired of being looked at all the time.'"

"You never say anything," Kendra observed. "It's freaky."

I turned down the corner of my page and returned her obstinate gaze. "What do you want me to say?"

"I don't know. *Something.* What is it with you and these books?"

"I like reading. Since when is that a crime?"

Kendra sat down on the adjacent bed and began to thread the laces through her bright, white, and thoroughly unsmudged Keds. "It's just kind of stuffy and middle-aged."

Winnie was now explaining to the stranger in the yellow suit that her family had lived in Treegap forever—since before any other families lived there—and she recounted her grandmother's tale that the town around them had been "all trees once, just one big forest . . . but it's mostly all cut down now. Except for the wood." Was it possible that Winnie Foster was telling my story also? I too was an only child, living under the close scrutiny of my overbearing parents. I too grew up in a neighborhood (much like a small town) that had once been nothing but trees on a bluff above miles of sea. My grandmother lived there also, and she remembered moving into her house in 1953 before much of the area had been occupied, before Fauntleroy had become what is commonly known today as a "suburb," where—despite its dwindling sense of seclusion—settlers still seek refuge from the urban world.

I wanted to stay in the room and keep reading. I had to know the outcome of Winnie's plot to run away, and of course I was interested also in the Tuck family, who had found—it would seem—the fountain of youth in the woods near Winnie's home, and as a consequence of drinking from it, were now immortal and had not aged a bit in eighty-seven years. But, in true storybook fashion, there came a knock at the door, and Kendra and I were summoned outside for the first of our Encounter Sessions.

"As you all know, part of this weekend's experience involves working in small groups with some of your peers and one of our gracious chaperones. As I call your name, please line up next to the adult to whom you have been assigned." Miss Christjaener proceeded down the roster but failed to call my name. I listened closely, yet it was never read. Did this mean I was exempt from participating? Perhaps I could sneak back to my crackerbox bedroom, dive into the comfort of the new book, and no one would be the wiser. As the groups dispersed, I trailed along quietly, hoping to veer off at the next bend in the hall.

"Julie!" Miss Christjaener exclaimed. "You're not on my list. Where are you going?" A dozen heads snapped around and stared.

I shrugged. "I'm not sure."

"It must have been an oversight. I don't know how we missed you. Here—you go with Dave Hemme's group." She directed me toward the man with the bulldog face, sagging jowls, and the droopiest, saddest eyes I had ever seen.

≈

Outside in the cool grass, we formed a circle, crossing our legs so that our knees were nearly touching. I don't remember the other children in my group. I remember only Mr. Hemme, whose premature arthritis was flaring up again, so he sat in a lawn chair with a crescent of prepubescents at his feet.

"We're supposed to"—he cleared his throat loudly—"*inspire* you with some kind of—personal testimony. I don't know if I can really do that, but I'll try. Some of you may have seen me around at church. You probably know my daughter—Sarah—or my other daughter—Mary—since they go to your school. I have another daughter in college, and a son who dropped out to go to Vo-Tech, and I'm married. My wife made some of your cheerleading uniforms, so you might have met her then."

Dave Hemme was a large man, crammed tightly in a chair made for someone much smaller. He was about my father's height but broader across the shoulders and with a large stomach that protruded over the waist of his pants. I also noticed his sideburns came down a bit too far, while the hair on top of his head had been clipped short, almost military-style. His cheeks were clean-shaven, but his skin had a scratchy look about it, and there were huge pockets under his eyes, which seemed the result of consistent sleep deprivation.

"What else about me?" he murmured. "Well, I'm a math teacher. I like math. I've always liked it. It always just came natural to me, I guess, and it's easier to like something when you're good at it. But even though I get involved with the numbers and working out the equations, showing other people how to do it, I've always had this—this nagging feeling that my life is incomplete; that I'm just walking on eggshells, just biding my time. I guess you could call it a *void*. And nothing and no one can fill it for me: not my wife, my kids, my work, nothing. I'm not even sure if God can."

Now my ears perked up. This was a first time I had ever heard a declaration of doubt from a grown person toward God. Certainly my father would never admit such a thing, even if he had wavered before.

"The truth is, I probably shouldn't be here." He looked around nervously, as if expecting a spotlight or video surveillance camera. "I mean, *here*, at this retreat, telling you my story about—spiritual crisis and recovery—and I mean, *here*, on this planet. I'm a mathematician, and the odds are against it that I should be here at all now." He took a deep breath, let it out slowly, and the chair creaked with him as he said: "In the last eighteen months, I've tried to kill myself no less than six times."

A terrible silence swept over us. I had kept a growing tally in my head for years of different kinds of falls—the apple on Newton's head, Niagara, succumbing to temptation, falling asleep, in love, over a cliff, into the arms of someone, boys playing football on the playground (who weren't afraid their insides might be horribly jostled around, their bodies permanently damaged . . . )—but this was the first time I knew distinctly what it meant to say *a hush had fallen*. I felt reverent toward the moment, averting my eyes to the ground. When I looked up again, I saw that Mr. Hemme was crying, silently—and his whole body trembled with each tear.

At last, he continued: "Sometimes it's hard for me to concentrate on anything but death. I know it's coming, one way or another, but I don't always want to fight it. Does that make sense?"

For the first time, I think he remembered his audience. I met his eyes and nodded. "I want to have some say in something, and I've never liked the notion of borrowed time, here on God's dime, that sort of thing. So every night on the way home from work, I stop off at this place. I think it's a kind of lover's lane, but no one's around at that time of night . . . not during rush hour. And I sit there in my car, and I know I'm supposed to be going to my support group for Suicide Survivors and the Christian Men's Group and my therapist and taking all these pills for depression, the numbness I feel toward the world . . . but I resist it, all of it. I sit in my car, and I fantasize about driving over that ledge, plummeting down into the ravine, going out in a great blaze of glory. . . . Do you want to know the only thing holding me back?"

He seemed to be speaking directly to me now, with an intensity I feared and cherished. "It isn't God and my faith in him. It isn't even my kids or the thought of obligation to my family. It is just plain fear. Not fear of death either—fear of *not dying*, being stuck in that car with both my legs broke, helpless and in pain and no way out. But if I could be guaranteed that I would die instantly, that I wouldn't have to suffer anymore . . . "

He shook his head, wiped his face with a thin white handkerchief, and looked out over us and across the field into the woods. "If God would make me that promise, I'd drive up there right now and end it all."

Lexicon-building: *Thanatos*, from the Greek for "Death" and the personification of this figure. In Greek mythology, Thanatos is the twin brother of Hypnos, the personification of Sleep, suggesting that death and sleep are closely related. In psychoanalytic terms, the word suggests a primitive desire for destruction and decay. This "death wish" or "death instinct" coexists in human beings with an instinct for life or survival.

While Kendra is in the shower later that night, I attempt a prayer for Dave Hemme. I kneel down on the linoleum floor, my nightgown tucked under my knees as a makeshift cushion. I bow my head and interlace my fingers and try very hard—as the pastor taught us—to "say what is in my heart."

"God, do you remember last year when I memorized the 'To Be or Not to Be' monologue from *Hamlet* for drama class? I didn't really think about what I was saying, what the words meant all together as a speech. At the time, it only mattered that I knew what word came next and next and next, so I could get through the whole thing without messing up. But tonight when Mr. Hemme was talking, he was doing a version of the same speech. Not exactly *the same*, I guess, because Hamlet seems more afraid of what comes after death, and Dave Hemme seems more afraid of all that comes before, but it amounts to the same kind of despair, doesn't it? No one understands how to live *or* how to die, but we are doing both all the time. And that's called a *paradox*, which is one of the best words I know, and a word that applies to almost every situation. But I get it now, God. We're in a no-win situation down here.

"*To die, to sleep—No more; and by a sleep to say we end/The heart-ache and the thousand natural shocks/That flesh is heir to—'tis a consummation/Devoutly to be wish'd.*" So sleep is like death, but to die is also to say good-bye to sleep forever—to go *beyond* sleep, beyond even coma. Some part of us must always want to surrender. We're tired of the burden of bodies, of being *sentient*, which is another vocabulary word I've recently learned meaning *capable* of experiencing pleasure and pain. As if it's a special gift or something. Only humans and animals are sentient beings, and only humans seem unsure how to feel about *having* this capacity to feel. That's a paradox, too. But then Hamlet—but really William Shakespeare—says it again: *To die, to sleep*, but this time—*To sleep, perchance to dream. Ay, there's the rub.* I never understood that part, unless it means that dreams rub against our minds and challenge what it is we think we already know. Maybe dreams cause friction between our waking selves and our sleeping selves, turning us into *somnambulists*, which is a word I've learned on my own. Maybe all of us are just two different people with two different sets of desires.

But then the speech goes on: *For in that sleep of death what dreams may come*, which I guess could be referring to the Afterlife or might mean that Heaven itself is just a dream, in the illusion sense of the word. But the part that always intrigued me from the whole soliloquy is this idea of the "mortal coil." *When we have shuffled off this mortal coil,/Must give us pause.*

If shuffling it off is another way of saying "dying," what is the coil itself? Is it the skin, the body, the shell? And what *are* we without this coil—are we naked or homeless? Dead or alive?

I had just read in my science book that turtles would probably live forever if it weren't for "human factors." But we are the human factors, and if we want to stop living, shouldn't we have the right to stop? And if we want to keep going, *how* exactly should we keep going? There's no textbook for any of this because if there were, believe me, I would have checked it out with my library card.

Now Kendra returns carrying her basket of assorted soaps and shampoos, a skimpy towel cinched under her arms, and I look bashfully away. "Who were you talking to in here?" she demands. "And why does it smell bad? Did you fart?"

"No," I say, still averting my eyes and slipping quickly under the covers. "I'm just going to read for a while, but I brought my book light, so it's OK if you want to go to sleep."

"*Sleep*? Are you kidding? A bunch of us are going over to the boys' dorm to throw rocks at their windows. Wanna come?"

"Thanks, but I think I'd rather stay here."

I can't see her face, but I imagine she is rolling her eyes and playing with her hair. "Big surprise!" Soon, she is out the door in a flash of cutoff shorts and brightly colored sweatshirt.

The central question of *Tuck Everlasting* is also one of to be or not to be. I am beginning to wonder whether there is any other kind of question, and if there is, whether such a question is even worth considering. Like Winnie, I have been effectively kidnapped by this extended weekend away, and also like Winnie, I'm not entirely sure I mind. There is something of the otherworld about this place as well, and though the bed is too short for my long body and the mattress too lean for my preference, I settle into it, resolving to finish the book—with its meager one hundred thirty-nine pages—before I shove off to sleep.

It's a profound book based on the problem of choices. The Tuck family never made the choice to drink from the Immortality Fountain. They were thirsty in the woods and came upon a gentle spring. For them, it was a matter of convenience—the way I've always thought it must have been for Adam and

Eve with the delectable spectacle of the fruit. Later, as they discovered they weren't growing older and that nothing could hurt them, they remembered the spring and began to assemble their story. Now Winnie comes along, and she is curious. In this way, we are also the same. And she sees Jesse, who will be forever seventeen even though he is really a hundred and four, drinking from the spring, and she wants to drink from it too. So his story must be relayed to her, and she must be made to see how dangerous the prospect of immortality would be—preserving her as a girl of ten forever.

So the reader is invited to consider what she would choose in a similar situation. What would life mean if there were no threat of death, no possibility of harm? Is it the turtle and the shell again? Is life even life without the certainty that it is temporary, and therefore fragile, and therefore precious somehow? When you remove the risk, do you eliminate the potential value of the action? I can't decide, and Winnie can't decide, but before the story's end, Jesse has given her a bottle of spring water, suggesting that—when she is seventeen—she might drink from it also and spend a youthful eternity with him.

There are two particularly curious outcomes of this story, neither of which can be described as purely "happy" or purely "tragic." *Poignant* seems the most appropriate word. Winnie has the impulse to save someone—or something; to use her newfound power to effect a change. The paradox, of course, is that the change she chooses to effect is one of changelessness: "In a moment she was back again. The toad still squatted where she had dropped it, the dog still waited at the fence. Winnie pulled out the cork from the mouth of the bottle, and kneeling, she poured the precious water, very slowly and carefully, over the toad. . . . Winnie smiled. Then she stopped and put her hand through the fence and set the toad free. 'There!' she said. 'You're safe. Forever.'"

That, it seemed to me, was a lovely sentiment. I had a notion that if I had a bottle filled with water from that spring, I might have taken it over to Mr. Hemme's room in the boys' dormitory and doused his head with it—a strange and prophetic baptism. And when he woke in a fright, not knowing yet that his fate had changed, that his path had been unswervingly altered, I would be inclined to say something coy, something like my mother always said: "There. You'll just have to live with it." And in this way, immortality might not equal changelessness at all but an opportunity for exceptional revelation.

The book's epilogue also stirred this feeling, the not-quite-sure-what-to-make-of-it feeling, and the further sense that I was in the presence of something phantasmal but true. Many years later, the everlasting Tucks return to Treegap. No one knows for sure what Winnie has done with her life—if she has drunk from the spring to safeguard her future or relinquished Forever in favor of Something Else. To be or not to be . . . *eternally.*

In the cemetery, the Tucks find her headstone. "In Loving Memory/Winnifred Foster Jackson/Dear Wife/Dear Mother/1870–1948," it reads. And so we, the reader-watchers, know what she has chosen without ever seeing the consequences of this choice, its pleasures and pains, her most private moments of sentient certainty and sentient regret. I imagine she ran to the spring on many occasions, unpiled the little monument of stones, and poised her lips to drink. Who wouldn't want the freedom to wander aimlessly through traffic? To dive into any depth of water? Who wouldn't wonder if Sarah Hodson emerged from the coma alive? (She did, but altered . . . ) And can anything more be said of anyone else than that he went on until he didn't, that she emerged as herself but different?

I can hear the girls whooping now and running through the damp grass, the boys bellowing behind them, their chorus shattering the night's calm. But I like best this interpretation of the story, and more stories than just this one: "'Pa thinks it's something left over from—well, some other plan for the way the world should be,' said Jesse. 'Some plan that didn't work out too good. And so everything was changed.'"

# Acknowledgments

## Personal Acknowledgments

It is with immense gratitude that I acknowledge the following people for their contributions to my life and work.

From the beginning: my grandmother, June Marion Wade (1911–2008), and my aunt, Linda Ann Wade (1945–2004). Also, early on: April Davis, Linda Breuer, Vanessa Ortblad, Anna Murray, Kathe Curran, Carolyn Du Pen, Sally McLaughlin, Sister Rosemary Perisich, and Sister Janice Holkup.

From Pacific Lutheran University: David Seal, for that first beret toss and everything after; my inspiring teachers, Beth Kraig, Patsy Maloney, Barbara Temple-Thurston, Charles Mudede, and Christine Moon; also, Ben Dobyns, Becky Farrell, Kara Larson, and all my friends from Saxifrage—*no ideas but in things!*

From Western Washington University: my mentors in composition, Donna Qualley, Bill Smith, and Star Rush; my mentors in literature, Bruce Beasley, Steve Vanderstaay, Suzanne Paola, and Brenda Miller—who also introduced me to my first lyric essays.

From University of Pittsburgh: Kathryn Flannery, Lucy Fischer, and Lisa Parker, three exceptional mentors and enduring friends.

From Carnegie Mellon University: the Department of Social and Decision Sciences, especially my dear friends, Amy Patterson, John Miller, and Connie Angermeier, and my favorite "mad scientist," Robyn Dawes.

Thanks also to my friends in 208C and elsewhere in Steel City: Katie Hogan, Gabe Yu, Mandy Holbrook, Sarah Scholl, Kerry Reynolds, and Fatin Abdal-Sabur.

From University of Louisville: my colleagues in the GTA office—for their constant camaraderie; "the Lunas"—Carol Stewart, Amy Tudor, Rev Culver, and Sara Northerner—exceptional in all things; and for my first friend in Derby City, James Leary—

a true friend at that. Particular gratitude goes to Annette Allen and Paul Griner for their vast knowledge and vigilant kindness.

Thanks to my "outlaws," Kim and Matt Striegel, for welcoming me years ago into your family; for my niece, Evie, and my new nephew, Nolan "Hondo" Striegel, whose birth coincided with the happy event of this book.

Thanks to my students, past, present, and yet to come—most especially my students at Olney Friends School, from whom I learned so much. Many good wishes to Keely Lewis, with admiration for all you are and all you will become.

Thanks to my dear mentor and friend, Steve VanderStaay, for writing the book description that appears on the cover flaps.

Special thanks are due to my incomparable friends and first readers, for your faith in me and for your unflagging endurance—Anna Rhodes, Tom Campbell, Dana Anderson, James Allen Hall, and Helena Studer. I am better for having known you.

Most of all, I want to thank my partner, Angie Griffin, for eight extraordinary years. *Amor vincit omnia.*

## Literary Acknowledgments

Many of the lyric essays in this collection, sometimes in slightly altered form, have been previously published or otherwise acknowledged by literary journals. Many thanks to the editors and judges of these literary journals and contests for their support.

**Wishbone** was named Honorable Mention for the 2006 *Gulf Coast* Nonfiction Prize by John D'Agata. This acknowledgment was made in Vol. 19, No. 1, the Winter/Spring 2006 issue of *Gulf Coast Journal of Literature and Fine Art.*

**Dreaming in Alpha** appears in *Cream City Review*, Vol. 30, No. 2, 2006, dedicated to "Surreal Memoir."

**Early Elegies** was named a Finalist for the 2005 Iowa Award in Nonfiction. It appears in the Fall 2008 issue of *Fifth Wednesday Journal,* and is a 2009 Pushcart Prize nominee.

**Third Door** appears in *Southeast Review,* Vol. 25, No. 2, 2007.

**A Life under Water** was named a Finalist for the 2007 *Arts & Letters* Nonfiction Prize. It received the 2009 AWP Intro Journals Award for Nonfiction and is forthcoming from *Tampa Review* in 2010.

**A Life on Land** was named a Finalist for the 2008 *Arts & Letters* Nonfiction Prize.

**Black Fleece** was awarded the 2004 *Gulf Coast* Nonfiction Prize by Mark Doty. It appears in *Gulf Coast Journal of Literature and Fine Art,* Vol. 17, No. 1, Winter/Spring 2005, and was subsequently nominated for a Pushcart Prize.

**Meditation 26** was awarded the 2006 Literal Latte Ames Essay Award. It appears in the Summer 2007 issue of *Literal Latte* online.

**Bouquet** appears in the Fall 2006 issue of *Third Coast.*

**Carapace** appears in *Alaska Quarterly Review,* Vol. 25, Nos. 3 & 4, 2008.

# Notes

## Wishbone

The song lyrics that begin "Moons and Junes and Ferris wheels" are from Joni Mitchell, "Both Sides Now," *Both Sides Now* (New York: Warner Bros., 2000). (compact disc)

The song lyrics that begin "This is your new thing now" are from Shawn Colvin, "New Thing Now," *A Few Small Repairs* (New York: Columbia Records, 1996). (compact disc)

The line of poetry, "The way things work is eventually something catches," is from Jorie Graham, "The Way Things Work," *Hybrids of Plants and of Ghosts* (Princeton, NJ: Princeton University Press, 1980).

The song lyrics that begin "The world still is the same" are from "You're Nobody Till Somebody Loves You," © Russ Morgan, Larry Stock, and James Cavanaugh, Shapiro Bernstein & Co., Inc., Memory Lane Music Group, 1944.

The song lyrics that begin "I won't forget when Peter Pan" are from Dar Williams, "When I Was a Boy," *The Honesty Room* (New York Razor & Tie, 1995). (compact disc)

The song lyrics that begin "Isn't it rich?" are from "Send in the Clowns," © Stephen Sondheim, from the 1973 musical *A Little Night Music*.

The line of poetry, "Nature's first green is gold," is from Robert Frost, "Nothing Gold Can Stay," *The Poetry of Robert Frost*, Complete and Unabridged (New York: Henry Holt and Company, 1969).

## Dreaming in Alpha

The line "sapphires in the mud" refers to T. S. Eliot's poem "Burnt Norton," from *The Four Quartets* (1944) (New York: Harvest Books, 1968).

The line "J. D.'s masterpiece" refers to the novel *The Catcher in the Rye*, by J. D. Salinger (1951) (Boston: Back Bay Books, 2001).

The line "write it like disaster" refers to Elizabeth Bishop's poem "One Art," from *The Complete Poems, 1927–1979* (New York: Farrar, Straus and Giroux, 1984).

### A Life under Water

The epigraph is from Adrienne Rich, "Diving into the Wreck," *Diving into the Wreck, Poems: 1971–1972* (New York: Norton, 1994).

Information about Anaximander is from to B. R. Hergenhahn, *An Introduction to the History of Psychology*, 4th ed. (Belmont, CA: Wadsworth, 2001).

The poem "Blue Love" is credited gratefully to my friend, Ben Dobyns.

### A Life on Land

The line of poetry "The longing is to be pure; what you get is to be changed" is from Jorie Graham, "Disenchantment," *Overlord* (New York: Ecco Press, 2006).

### Black Fleece

The epigraph is from Mary Oliver from her book-length poem, *The Leaf and the Cloud*, as is the poetic interlude that begins, "Bless the fingers, for they are as darting as fire . . ." (Cambridge, MA: Da Capo Press, 2001).

### Meditation 26

This essay relies on seven epigraphs from the following sources:

First is from the familiar childhood prayer "Now I Lay Me Down to Sleep."

Second is from Marilyn Hacker's poem "Dusk: July," *Winter Hours: Poems* (New York: Norton, 1996).

Third is from Susanne Antonetta's book *A Mind Apart: Travels in a Neurodiverse World* (Los Angeles: J. P. Tarcher, 2005).

Fourth is from Jorie Graham's poem "Prayer," *Never* (New York Ecco Press, 2003).

Fifth is from John Donne's "Meditation 17" (1623), *Devotions Upon Emergent Occasions and Death's Duel* (New York: Cosimo Classics, 2007).

Sixth is from Naomi Shihab Nye's poem "How Palestinians Keep Warm," *Red Suitcase* (Rochester, NY: BOA Editions, 1994).

Seventh is from Emily Dickinson's "Poem 167," *The Complete Poems of Emily Dickinson* (Boston: Back Bay Books, 1976).

The refrain *All those deaths I've crossed on straw* is from Paul Eluard, "I Love You (Je t'aime)" (1946–1951), *Last Love Poems of Paul Eluard*, translated by Marilyn Kallet (Boston: Black Widow Press, 2006).

### Bouquet

Research into the nomenclature and characteristics of wildflowers is credited to the many Master Gardeners I have known since childhood as well as to the valuable information provided by the following websites: http://www.wildflowerinformation.org and http://www.flowers.org.uk/flowers/facts/common-names.htm

### Carapace

The "Humpty Dumpty" nursery rhyme is credited to Roud Folk Song Index #13026.

The story "The Legend of Sleepy Hollow" is from Washington Irving, *The Legend of Sleepy Hollow* (1920) (New York: Atheneum, 2007).

Excerpted material from *Joni: An Unforgettable Story* is from Joni Eareckson, *Joni: An Unforgettable Story* (Billy Graham Evangelical, Special Crusade Edition, 1976).

Excerpted material from *Tuck Everlasting* is from Natalie Babbitt, *Tuck Everlasting* (New York: Farrar, Straus and Giroux, 1988).

Excerpted material from *Hamlet* is credited to William Shakespeare, *Hamlet* (1600) (New York: Simon & Schuster, 2003).